ALSO BY CARL A. HAMMERSCHLAG, M.D.

▲

THE DANCING HEALERS

CARL A.
HAMMERSCHLAG, M.D.

THE THEFT OF THE SPIRIT

A JOURNEY

TO SPIRITUAL

HEALING

A FIRESIDE BOOK

PUBLISHED BY SIMON & SCHUSTER

NEW YORK LONDON TORONTO SYDNEY TOKYO SINGAPORE

F

FIRESIDE
Rockefeller Center
1230 Avenue of the Americas
New York, New York 10020

First Fireside Edition 1994

FIRESIDE and colophon are registered trademarks
of Simon & Schuster Inc.

Designed by Songhee Kim
Manufactured in the United States of America

5 7 9 10 8 6 4

Library of Congress Cataloging-in-Publication Data

Hammerschlag, Carl A.
The theft of the spirit : a journey to spiritual healing / Carl A.
Hammerschlag.
p.   cm.
1. Healing—Psychological aspects. 2. Ritual—Therapeutic use.
3. Spiritual healing. 4. Holistic medicine. 5. Psychosomatic medicine.
6. Indians of North America—Medicine.   I. Title.
R726.5.H33   1993
615.8'52'08997—dc20   93-19036
                                                                         CIP

ISBN 0-671-88553-7

The poem on page 130 is reprinted from *Time Dollars*,
copyright © 1992 by Rodale Press.
Permission granted by Rodale Press, Inc., Emmaus, PA 18098.

DEDICATION

▲

To All My Relations

To Bill and Vera Tyner, who taught me how to pray and
whose love for each other and for all their relations
is still with us as a living benediction.
To Evangeline Talaheftewa, faithkeeper.
To Sigmund Freud, Carl Jung, and Milton Erickson,
who transcended dogma.
To Joseph Campbell, who knew that the meaning of life
was in the experience of it.
To Mahatma Gandhi, whose prescription for living
with joy has not been improved upon: "If you're going
to be somewhere, be there."
To my mother, who only wanted me to hang my shingle
down the block from her and who ultimately said,
Do what you want.
To my daughters, Lisa, Amy, and Tara,
who have steadfastly refused to differentiate the
public me from the ordinary airbag I also am.
To Elaine, my fellow-traveling soulmate.
And to each of you; you know who you are.
You fill my cup with joy.

▲

CONTENTS

▲

▲

THE THEFT OF THE SPIRIT

▲

INTRODUCTION

⏶

O nce upon a time, before technology and endless years of formal education had made us so smart, and before we became preoccupied with material wealth, we learned what mattered most in our lives by living in communities, intertwined with the people around us. They told us their stories; we told them ours. All the stories were unique, yet ultimately they were all the same. They still are the same. They're about hope and fear, pain and deliverance. They help us make sense of our own lives, give us hope . . . heal our souls.

Stories touch us because we can feel the storyteller's spirit in the telling. Stories help us make sense of our experiences and move beyond our preconceptions. We don't listen to stories much anymore in this era of instant communication, so it's hard to really feel the spirit of the teller.

I learned a lot in universities, got plenty of degrees, and thought I knew a lot, but I kept learning the things that really matter over

⏶

and over again until I knew them in my unconscious mind, in my blood, in my dreams, in that place beyond thought. I was reasonably well trained in the science of medicine, but that didn't make me a healer. It was through stories, those of my patients and my teachers, that I became a healer. And what those stories taught me is now told in the language of a new science called psychoneuroimmunology (PNI), a medical specialty that says the mind, body, and spirit are chemically connected and that what you know matters less than what you feel. It's not that psychoneuroimmunologists dismiss traditional medical knowledge; rather, we're learning that it may not be the most important criterion for living effectively. Now we can see our stories in chemical equations that tell us that how we feel in our hearts and souls changes all kinds of measures of immunologic strength. If you're happy and have faith, belief, and purpose, you can cope better with whatever mental, physical, or emotional challenges you face than if you're depressed, frightened, and mistrustful.

This book is the story of my metamorphosis from doctor to healer, from doer to helper. It's a story of an arrogant young physician who was sent to New Mexico to fulfill his military obligation by working with Native Americans. I knew nothing about Indians other than what I'd seen in the movies and thought that cheering for them would give me an inside track to acceptance. It didn't. I was a "white man" and, therefore, held responsible for centuries of depredations of the Indian people even though I myself wasn't culpable. It served as a reminder of my own judgments, particularly my attitude toward Germans, an inner poison that I'd never acknowledged needed to be drained.

▲

INTRODUCTION

I've stayed in Indian country as a physician for most of my life. It was there that I began to learn about methods of healing I'd never imagined possible and about an energy source within us that can help renew us, especially at those times when we need it most. There I also learned stories about journeying past fear and illusion and getting beyond all the garbage we acquire as we struggle along alone.

This is a book about ordinary people, some of whose names I've changed. They're extraordinary ordinary people who looked within so they didn't have to do without, people who didn't choose to abandon their dreams because others considered them improbable.

I hope this book helps you on your journey. Maybe you'll find a story in it that touches your dream, or one that nurtures your spirit.

I wish you joy on your journey and stories to tell.

▲

PROLOGUE

━━━━━━━━━━━━━━━━━━▲━━━━━━━━━━━━━━━━━━

I n northern Arizona, at the southern end of the Tusayan Plateau,
is Black Mesa. At its end, the mesa splits into three precipi-
tous cliffs on which about a dozen Hopi villages sit. Of these,
among the oldest is Shongopovi, a "grandfather village."

Until recently, this village was the only one of the reservation's
twelve communities that still practiced the entire traditional twelve-
month cycle of religious ceremonies. But in the late 1970s, the ceremonial calendar was disrupted because of a theft. The village's
most precious religious symbol was stolen, and because of this
loss, hundreds of men still await initiation into tribal adulthood.

The villages on Black Mesa represent close to a thousand years
of uninterrupted survival in a tradition of peace. Despite savageries
unleashed by warrior tribes, conquistadors, or those who came
after, and despite attempts to disrupt their traditions, the Hopi as
a nation were never dissuaded from their spiritual commitment to

━━━━━━━━━━━━━━━━━━▲━━━━━━━━━━━━━━━━━━

the traditional way of harmony with the earth that is the predicate
for their survival.

The word *Hopi* means peaceful, but it also means to obey and
have faith in the instructions of the Great Spirit. To be Hopi means
not to distort any of the teachings for influence or power, or in any
other way to corrupt the Hopi way of life. Otherwise, the name
would be taken away from the people.

Yet from their ancient prophecies, the Hopi have always known
that many would turn away from the "life plan" given by the Creator, Masauu, and that some would abandon the ceremonial duties that governed their lives. Then blood would flow, followed by
endless disasters—earthquakes and floods, changes in the weather
and the seasons, and the disappearance of wildlife. Then there
would come a time for either purification or destruction.

Over the years, the Hopi tradition has resisted the social disin-
tegration that has been the fate of so many tribes because it is
flexible enough to accommodate some outside influences. At the
same time, the Hopi are so certain of their place on earth that they
can maintain their own integrity as a tribe in the face of many
changes.

My mentor and spiritual guide, the late Herbert Talaheftewa, a
traditional clan chief, came from Shongopovi. He was leader of
the Two Horn Society, the religious group responsible for the ceremony initiating young Hopi men into manhood. Since the beginning of time—according to Hopi stories, since their migration
to this place on the mesa—Hopi children have looked forward to
two special initiation ceremonies. These magnificent communal

PROLOGUE

events, with song, dance, prayer, sacred ritual, and secrets, bond these people to each other, to their land, and most of all, to the Creative Source. This celebration allows for their perpetuity as a people.

The first initiation ceremony takes place when a boy is about six and it begins the young Hopi's ceremonial career. It is here that members of the Hopi nation learn the stories of their history, of their emergence into this world, of the values that sustain them. They learn clearly their specific roles in spiritual and community life so that each can speak with the other and then they can stand together as one people.

Unlike contemporary non-Indian society, where children are allowed only limited freedom in childhood and then increasing freedom as they get older, in Hopi life the opposite is true. Children come and go as they please and their only restrictions are those they learn from experience. As they get older, more is expected of them as their participation in the religious life of the community is prescribed.

The second initiation, which takes place between ages eighteen and twenty-five, is more secret and more crucial because it moves the neophyte into full maturity as one of "the people," a keeper of a faith that allows the world to stay in balance. Without this initiation ceremony, one cannot fully participate in the religious and cultural life of the community. It is the culture's single most important rite of passage.

At the heart of this manhood initiation ceremony in the village of Shongopovi are the three sacred symbols affectionately called the Children. The physical presence of the objects—three hu-

18

manlike figures made of wood, known formally as Talaotimsi (male and female figure) and Avachmana—is an absolute requirement for this rite of passage. These sacred totemic objects, estimated to be two thousand years old, empower the event. Without them, the ceremony is inauthentic and unacceptable. Without them, it cannot take place. And without fully initiated members to conduct the sacred ceremonies, the Hopi way of life cannot continue.

Just prior to Herbert's death from heart disease in 1979, the Children were discovered missing. That, I think, is part of what broke his heart.

I am standing on the edge of Shongopovi village, looking down on the graveyard below. Herbert's grave is under one of those piles of sand and stone covered with pottery shards and baskets. There is no marker. A raven cries and I feel my own sadness. An hour ago, I sat with Herbert's wife. I call her So'oh (Grandmother). It was she who told me about the theft of the Children. Tearfully, she said, "One of us did it. If the sacred figures are not found, the Hopi will die as a nation."

Never in history has a single theft wiped out an entire people. Through adversity in warfare, torture, famine, drought, and pestilence, the Hopi have not been annihilated, but the theft of their spirit has sown the seeds of their elimination, bringing the prophesied end that much closer.

Even though I knew what this loss signified to the Hopi, as I listened to So'oh, I still thought, "What's the big deal?" These effigies are pieces of wood, each maybe thirty inches long. Two of them look like the spokes of a wagon wheel with a painted face on one end. The male's is pale blue, the female's, reddish. The third is about the same length with three interlocking legs and a small, round carved ocher head.

"Why not just carve some new figures and get on with the program?" I thought. I mean, we're talking about life and death here. I come from a people whose life-sustaining totemic object is a book, not an image. If a book wears out, you print another edition and keep it going! We have a sacred obligation to tell our children the story so they can tell it to their children and on and on. So I tried to tell her, "If it's not the *exact* piece of wood, at least you still remember the songs, you still know the dances in the right order and in the exact way." I wanted to leave, to walk away from her painful sorrow if I could not convince her. "Give me a break, So'oh," I said. "You must go on without them. Something is better than nothing. You must continue to initiate."

But So'oh said, "No, you've misunderstood. It's not only the old pieces themselves that matter so much. We are selling our birthrights. Since the dawn of time, the Creator's plan was for the Hopi to keep their identity. It was prophesied that the influence of white people would yield a disappearance of sacred land and objects. The loss of the Children is a sign of a much bigger crisis.

"I have nieces and nephews who speak only English. We cannot practice our religion if we don't understand our language. Once our religion is gone, nothing will bring it back. We will not be Hopis anymore. We will not know who we are."

So'oh believes a Hopi stole the pieces and sold them to feed his

▲

alcohol addiction. And if a Hopi can sacrifice his people's essence for money, then their spiritual values have lost their meaning. The Hopi people will disappear because they have been unable to maintain these values. Like other spiritually bankrupt cultures, they have come to accept that everything has a price, even their souls.

"The Children give meaning to everything," So'oh told me patiently. "They provide an explanation for what can't be known. They remind us of the holiness in ourselves. If we submit to greed and temptation of material things, we will destroy ourselves. We will disappear into the underworld from which we came because we allowed the theft of our spirit."

And now I understand that a culture without symbols, rituals, or myth is a culture without morality. Stories, values, and symbols are the ways a culture shares its spiritual legacy. A culture that reveres life maintains its myths and symbols; without them, we dehumanize the life we live. A culture that upholds material wealth and technology as its only sustaining values worships death and stagnation. A culture that allows violence, materialism, and technology to determine its priorities devalues life and the spirit, and leaves no room for mystery, dreams, and growth.

The ease with which we excuse immorality today reinforces a belief that values can be replaced by objects. And that assumption erodes any understanding of what is right and wrong. Morality has become subordinate to expediency. Morality is deteriorating even more rapidly than our planet, which, as the Hopi have prophesied, is in the throes of an extinction spasm. This destruction will lead to the elimination of at least half the species on earth by

▲

the middle of the next century, and to the extinction of jungles, deserts, rain forests, and wetlands. Our indifference to the disappearance of these life forces not only irreversibly alters the physical atmosphere that supports life, but also causes the moral atmosphere to deteriorate.

Roy, So'oh's youngest son, recently visited the home of a well-known collector of Native American artifacts. A special room was fitted with subdued indirect lighting, piped-in music, and burning incense. When Roy approached the room, he had a premonition that he should not go inside. Something about it filled him with trepidation, but the collector encouraged him to go in and review the artifacts.

In the center of the room was a glass case, illuminated by an overhead spotlight that made it the room's central focus. Inside the case was the original headdress of the deity the Hopi call the Germinator. This mask is the symbolic embodiment of the Godhead itself. Roy felt unable to remain in the house and told his host that the mask did not belong there; it must be returned to the people who revered it. As Roy left, the collector called after him, "It is my most prized possession."

Today, our culture is *possessed* by *possession*! The Hopi know, as do all of us in our hearts, that civilization will come to an impoverished end when the spirit, or its symbols, are owned, not felt.

Since more than half of all the artifacts and art objects that the Hopi consider sacred have been stolen, religious leaders cannot pass on the knowledge of ceremonies, and there will be no qualified successors. These losses are equivalent to the destruction of

▲

the Wailing Wall, the burning of the True Cross, and the leveling of Mecca.

Thefts of sacred objects will continue if we allow reverence for life to be replaced in our hearts and our shared experience, by desire for money, possessions, and technology. Multiplication has taken precedence over sanctification. Truth is less valued than wealth and what is good is respected less than what is easy. The result is that the portion of ourselves that is imbued with spirit becomes faint and sick—and we, as a planet, become weaker.

When our history is written, let it not be said that we floundered because we allowed the theft of our spirit. There is still time.

1
RITUALS AND
CEREMONIES

Like the Hopi, we live in an age of growing disasters and increasing terrors, because as a civilization, we are disconnected from all those credible myths and norms that once sustained us. Without faith in a believable ethic, we suffer. The theft of spiritual meaning destroys us at every level—the individual, the family, the neighborhood, the culture, the nation, the fate of the world. The theft of the spirit disables us physically and emotionally.

What are the cultural myths that shape our world? Leaders of nations, business, and religion have been shown to be untrustworthy and unbelievable if not frankly criminal. Without any cultural or political guides who inspire trust, our perceptions of reality are created by sales professionals. Image has become more important than substance, and corruption has become commonplace, whether in government, medicine, law, or religion.

If self, technology, and possessions have become our pervasive

---

mythology, how can we reawaken in ourselves a sense of community that can sustain us? We can return to a life of morality through telling and listening to stories, through experiencing genuine awe, through participating in rituals and ceremonies. Each allows us to give expression to personal experience while connecting with our communities. We must reinvest our ceremonies and symbols with life-giving, healthful meaning. That is how we can make sense of our lives.

The enduring gift from Native Americans to us is the importance of ritual. Rituals and their symbols are the residue of culture. They invest the events in our lives with meaning. They illuminate and ultimately define our realities because they mark the milestones by which we define ourselves as individuals and as participants in a community. Without them, the potential richness of our lives loses its full depth and significance.

The core of a culture is a package of beliefs learned from childhood that makes the world coherent. When we speak of "reality," we are referring to that package. But we don't like to come to grips with how limited that world view usually is. For example, one of the myths of modern culture is its insistence that we can understand the universe. But even if we did understand what it is and how it began (cosmologists tell us that such a grand unifying theory is forthcoming), we would still be unable to answer the question of *why* it bothers to exist.

Since Western civilization seeks to explain all existence in terms of provable reality, we've learned to subordinate our feelings to the domination of reason. We've become afraid to express ourselves symbolically because the voices of the imagination generally fall outside scientific descriptions of reality. By cutting ourselves off in this way, we make it more difficult to deal with the disparity between our wishes and our realities.

Rituals and symbols can provide the structure by which life experiences yield new meaning. They help rediscover things you may need to see differently. For example, every year on Yom Kippur, the Jewish Day of Atonement, I wear the prayer shawl that I will be buried in. This yearly reminder of my mortality helps me stay in touch with my dreams. I spend the day wondering what I want to do with the rest of my life, contemplating last year's traumas and joys, and thinking about future choices. It's not that I don't think about these issues at other times, it's just that I don't ordinarily set aside time to create sacred space for their serious contemplation. It is through ritual that we separate our ordinary selves from our extraordinary possibilities and create the sacred time necessary to address important questions with the attention they deserve.

Throughout this book, you will hear stories about how ritual can guide us through crises by anchoring us in our spiritual truth; it can mark the important steps on the journey by highlighting the extraordinary. With such guidance, it becomes possible to see in new ways, to keep growing, to become the heroes of our own lives, to turn traumas into enlightenment, to clean up the garbage that burdens us—in short, to be free to live in truth.

Rituals have most power and meaning when they are shared in groups that reinforce the unity and community we need to sustain ourselves. But individuals can also develop personal rituals that are touchstones for their own truths.

To restore some healing myths to our own lives and to the world, we can revive old powerful rituals that have sustained peoples for centuries. And we can create new ones to meet the terrors of today.

Another of my mentors, Bill Dalton, created this ritual: Whenever I visited him, he would ask me an opening question. He would lean back on a wooden chair and, propped against the front of his one-room house on the White Mountain Apache reservation, he would ask:

"How come clover has three leaves? Why does the mountain lion's tail have a bush on its end? Why does the beetle always look down?" You get the picture. In a decade of questions, I never had the right answer.

I'd say, "The beetle always looks down because it is encased in a hard shell that is not hinged at the neck." *Wrong!*

The beetle looks down because at the time of creation, the Creator gave Beetle a most important task. When night fell, it was Beetle's job to carry the stars in a pail and place them, one by one, in the night sky.

One night, Beetle was late for his appointed rounds. Hurrying to get the job done, he carelessly stumbled and fell. The stars spilled out, which is how the Milky Way was formed. The Creator was so angry at Beetle's inattention that he made sure Beetle would always look down at the ground to watch his steps.

Every month on my arrival, Bill's grandkids and their friends would gleefully gather around the old man as he confronted me again with my stupidity. It got so that I'd drive around making sure no kids were there so I could avoid another round of public humiliation.

It turned out he didn't want "an" answer to any of the questions; he only wanted to see how long it took me to find other ways of responding. He would have been happy if I'd found an explanation in my imagination rather than seeking some "scientific" reason. Seeking an answer is the scientific paradigm; finding meaning is quite another. Bill was never impressed with my degrees; I was lucky he didn't hold them against me.

Bill always wanted me to look at things again. It's the same thing I tell my patients. If you really want to know something, look at it again. This message is ageless.

It's the message Moses got when he spoke to the Creator in front of the burning bush. Moses, awestruck by this demonstration of God's power, was told to take off his shoes because the ground upon which he stood was holy. Moses knew that the place was holy by this awesome display of divine power. Why did he have to take off his shoes? The commentaries on the Hebrew scriptures say it was a reminder that whenever you see something important, you can see it from another perspective if you step out of the ordinary and look again. When you can see from an extraordinary perspective, you will know that there is spirit in everything.

How many ways are there to see? As many ways as we are willing to look. Most of us spend so much time learning it one way that we develop a vested interest in only seeing it that way and getting others to see it the same way. That convinces us that the way we see it is really the way it is. This is the tenet on which most traditional educational systems are founded.

Most of us look only at what we already know, although what is most important to look at is what we often choose not to see. Every new discovery is born when someone takes a fresh look at something people thought they already knew. Creative breakthroughs and acts of genius are almost always considered acts of heresy; these acts challenge what is commonly known and force us to look again.

Rituals can provide a framework for helping us move beyond our impasses.

A close friend's second child was born blind. That fact was not firmly established until the child was several months old. One of the most dreadful fears of parents is: *What if, God forbid, my child is born deformed or retarded?* Friends and family were devastated by the news. Our concerns for both child and parents reflected our awareness that there, but for the grace of God, went we.

Howard and Sharona decided to sponsor a ritual gathering based on a Plains tribal tradition called the Talking Circle, which they had learned from me and our work together. Everyone comes to this ceremony believing he or she has something to say that somebody else needs to hear and that each of us needs to hear something that somebody else has to say. In the talking circle, everyone speaks from the heart, without interruption from the others.

The spontaneous speech that this type of ritual allows is close to prayer. Speech is a mind song, an expression that is processed by the brain before being articulated. Prayer is a heart song; it comes from the passion of the moment and is expressed without being judged as acceptable or worthy by the mind. The truth is always closer to the heart song; the heart knows things that the mind never even thought of because it has not yet become broken by doubt.

Together with friends and family, Howard and Sharona wanted to separate themselves from their old dreams and expectations about what this child was supposed to be, and accept their daughter and her specialness as a gift. They no longer wanted to burden Ariel or themselves with their fears and disappointments; instead, they wanted to start enjoying what she would teach them and what they would learn and achieve together.

They asked us to help them move into their current reality by first acknowledging our former wishes for what might have been and then focusing our energies on sharing, with the three of them, our joy, best wishes, and prayers. This gathering would be an act of liberation for us all.

In their living room, filled with people who love them, Howard and Sharona light an abalone shell filled with sage. We are cleansed of the ordinary dust of everyday life that clings to us by brushing ourselves with the fragrant smoke using an eagle feather. By preparing ourselves in this way, the Plains tribes say, thoughts and prayers are carried on the wings of eagles to touch the ear of God. This is a time for looking again. This is a new beginning, a liberation from preconceptions and old illusions.

The eagle feather is passed to each participant. One by one, each is given the opportunity to speak. Holding the feather, some speak for many minutes, some very briefly. No one is interrupted; there are no questions and no interpretations.

In the circle, I listen in a way different from that of a

▲

doctor. I'm not expected to provide interpretations or brilliant insight, so I really listen. I also speak differently, not thinking about what I'm going to say beforehand, trusting only that when the feather comes to me my heart will move my lips.

The parents hold the feather first. Howard says that he will give up his sadness about what this child could have been and will accept Ariel as she is. "She is a child with special qualities previously unimagined," he says. "She will be a source of inspiration and learning."

Sharona says she hopes all of us gathered together will experience with them the new possibilities about what can be.

One friend adds, "Ariel is blind, but she will see things the rest of us will never know. We who are sighted are often blind to that awareness."

Each of us, in our turn, takes the feather, and each one of us acknowledges our initial pain and now our relief. The way it is is the way it is. We each come to our friends with a common purpose, a pervasive sense of respect and love, the commitment of a community.

I used a version of the Talking Circle with Diana, a young woman who came to see me shortly after her boyfriend of five years committed suicide by carbon-monoxide poisoning in her garage. Ray had been violent, unstable, and abusive. More than once, he had threatened to kill Diana and then himself.

After the last violent confrontation, Diana left the house. In a fit of fury, Ray hammered in the roof of his car, placed a mattress in the indentation, and covered it with a blanket and pillow. With the car still parked in the garage, he turned on the ignition and climbed into his makeshift bed.

Diana had spent the night and next day at a girlfriend's house, too upset to go to work and afraid to go home unaccompanied. Together, the two women found Ray in the garage near the driver's door of his car, the keys in his hand and the ignition turned off. He had apparently changed his mind, but was so stuporous that he could not get out of the garage. Although he was still breathing when they found him, he had sustained such severe brain damage that subsequent swelling caused his brain stem to rupture through the base of his skull. He died several days later.

Diana was obviously confused—she felt pain, guilt, rage, and relief. And she felt responsible. Ray's parents, whom he despised, took his body back East for burial, but Diana needed a ritual that would allow her to express her feelings about this relationship and its tragic ending. I suggested that a Talking Circle might be appropriate. Together we planned a memorial service and she invited friends and family.

I explained the Talking Circle ritual, concluding with, "You can say anything you want; speak as long or briefly as you choose. Nobody will interrupt you, and when you're finished, simply pass the eagle feather." Each participant was asked to express his or her feelings in words. Some said that Ray's choice liberated Diana from his tyranny. Some were sad she was unable to take steps for her own health before the tragedy.

• • •

Diana tells her friends, "I just remembered that long ago I was given an eagle feather and I lost it. Maybe I couldn't fly away from Ray because I'd lost my feather. Maybe trying to take him with me kept me from flying free."

I say, "Ray's choice was his and choice is the greatest power. It is our ability to choose that liberates us. Diana, you can now choose to do penance for old transgressions or to seek absolution for sins real or imagined." I give her the eagle feather and remind her of the blessing from the book of Ecclesiastes: "To every thing there is a season and a purpose under heaven." As with the seasons, it's time to move on, maybe even to fly.

My own spiritual life is now intimately involved with Native American ceremonies. That is the "place" where I regularly and dependably touch that piece of my essence that reminds me I am connected to something other than myself. These rituals sustain me, they ignite my dreams, my belief in possibilities. It is in pursuing our dreams—of being something more than we are—that we are reminded of the power in our spirit.

In the summer of 1988, to celebrate my daughter's forthcoming marriage, I sponsored a Native American church ceremony in her honor. This special event launched her and her soon-to-be husband into their future with blessings and good wishes. They were the central focus of the nightlong ceremony. Whatever other issues people brought into the tipi with them were also dealt with, but the focus of attention was the new couple. People were there to share their prayers and hopes for their happiness and success.

▲

My daughter and future son-in-law knew only a few of the participants. They came because they knew it was important to me to bless them in that special place, the most prayerful place I know.

We went to the tipi grounds of my close friend (I call him brother) on the Gila River Reservation. Relatives from the Navajo, Pima, Mohave, Papago, and Havasupai tribes were present. They are people with whom I had prayed before; they are family.

Hours before the ceremony, I had broken a foot in a freak accident. At the time, I didn't realize my foot was broken, and it certainly didn't seem important enough to postpone the ceremony.

We line up outside the tipi and walk around it before entering. We sit to the immediate left of the Roadman, the spiritual leader. I introduce my children and say that I called this meeting to honor their marriage.

The Roadman says, "We are going to pray for this couple in the best ways we know how. Something good always happens when a man and woman come together in love. This coming together is the language of God, a reminder that this is the basic connection that sustains life. The songs we sing are prayers for your future."

The ceremonial staff is passed around and each one in the circle holds it with the left hand while holding the gourd rattle in the right hand. The Roadman continues, "This staff is the bow and the rattle with its fringes is the arrow. These songs are as powerful as arrows launched in warfare. Our words are carried in the smoke of tobacco and cedar raised on eagle wings to touch the ear of God. What-

▲

ever happens here tonight is going to be good, and when we all leave in the morning, we'll be renewed."

I feel wonderful, despite my throbbing foot and some nausea. The Roadman gives me more peyote, the sacred medicine, though I protest. He says there's something inside me that needs to come out.

I trust his wisdom, and as the hours of the ceremony pass, I learn what is inside. My broken foot is the acknowledgment of the loss of my daughter, whom I don't want to give away to this stranger. I'll cripple myself to keep from walking her down the aisle. For all their lives, I have unashamedly told my daughters that nobody would ever love them more—more unequivocally, more unjudgmentally—than their daddy. Now comes this man, who loves my daughter too. I won't share my jewel. I'd rather break my foot!

By the early morning, it is clear what needs to come out of me. In the tipi, I wear my father's prayer shawl. It is the most important tribal ritual object that I have. He wore it during his bar mitzvah in Germany more than fifty years ago. It was given to him by his father and it's one of the few things he brought with him when he escaped from the Nazis. I would have given it to my son, had he become a bar mitzvah. I feel my father's presence whenever I drape the shawl around me.

We have been up all night, and soon the morning sun will rise. I ask the Roadman if I can speak. I take off the shawl for the first time during a prayer service since my fa-

*ther placed it on my shoulders at my own bar mitzvah. I
had thought I did not have a son to give it to. Now I'm crying and I can hardly speak. At this moment, I see my
daughter clearly—not as a possession, but rather as a gift
loaned to me. I see that I no more raised her than she raised
me.*

*I walk over to this young man she loves and tell him I've
always wanted to share this prayer shawl with my son. I
place it on his shoulders and through his own tears says
he's never received a gift like this before.*

Thanks, Dad.

In the Native American tradition, there is no such designation as
in-law. Relationships are not decreed by law, they are made by
choice. I chose to make this young man my son, and if he's my son,
he's no longer an intruder.

The old Indians say that if you give away something that's important to you, your life is renewed. It means that *you* have the
things; the things don't have you. If you can't give away your possessions, they will destroy you. In ceremonies, such truths become clear, and we can truly see what our spirit needs.

Another kind of ritual has been created through a powerful symbol, the Vietnam Memorial Wall. This symbol has allowed many
Americans to feel forgiveness and to heal the wounds of a national
experience that left us all casualties.

For a long time I had an attitude about Vietnam. It was an im-
moral war. I demonstrated against it. I showered disdain upon returning veterans as if they were all complicitous baby killers. They

were the tools of a greedy military-industrial complex.

I did not then know that the realities experienced by the young Americans who went to Vietnam were as valid as mine. I believed that the way I saw it was the way it was. When I thought of 58,132 American soldiers dead, I felt only anger at the rhetoric about the "honor roll of heroes" and the tragedy that produced these needless losses. It was not until I had to treat returning Native American veterans with post-traumatic stress disorders that I chose to look again.

In proportion to their percentage in the population, American Indians have always been dramatically overrepresented in the military. When conflicts arise, they volunteer. It is the warrior tradition. Those who come from traditional homes and communities are blessed before leaving and strengthened by sacred objects they carry with them. On their return, they are blessed and cleansed from any lingering stain of the experience to be reintegrated into their communities.

For many who came back from Vietnam, *the rituals were not enough* to ease their reentry. As a nation, and as individuals, we did not greet the survivors of this war as returning heroes. There were no parades, no ticker tape, no applause from a grateful people. At home, they saw only a wish to push it all out of our memory, to pretend it hadn't happened.

But the veterans couldn't do that. I saw these young men kill themselves with self-inflicted gunshot wounds, by drugs and alcohol. I saw them beating wives, abusing children, and murdering in rage. I saw that I was part of the stone wall of denial they

▲

faced. It was one thing to be against the war, but I had confused the war with the warriors.

When the Vietnam Memorial was built in Washington, D.C., I vowed I would never go to see it. That was before I became immersed in the war's aftermath. Now I needed to go to The Wall. I needed to see the names, and I wanted to ask forgiveness.

It was after two o'clock in the morning when I asked the cabdriver to take me there. The destination didn't surprise him even at that hour.

I had only seen pictures of the monument. I was not prepared for it.

Names, names, names. First they appear at my feet as I stand on the grassy slope above the monument. Then I walk down to the V-shaped vertex. I stand ten feet below the base of the monument and all I see is names, names, names above and around me. And the mementos. I'm not prepared to see the faces. There are faces of boys in photographs laid on the ground, lit by candles that flicker in the night. By the light of a match, I read poems and letters from parents and lovers. A photograph with a handwritten note: "Our only son." Another photograph shows a private in combat uniform. Taken two weeks before he died, it's attached to a letter:

I see you now on a black wall, a name that I gave you
as I held you so close after you were born. As I held

you my hopes and dreams were of a good life for you, never dreaming of the few years we were to share. All that we loved ones can do now is to come here and remember. I remember you as a baby, I remember your first day at school, I remember the love we shared and I remember the day you died . . . I miss you so much and the hurt never ends. You are still with us in our hearts and if anyone reads this, I hope they will remember that each name they see here represents on the average of 20 years that each one was some mommy's little boy. So you are mine.

Love, Mom

With tears rolling down my cheeks, I put on my prayer shawl and skullcap to recite the lament for the dead. Then I walk slowly up the incline, touching my lips to the black quartz wall, and feeling each name etched on my brain.

Almost an hour later, pained, puffy-eyed, and silent, I find the same cabdriver exactly where I'd left him. He turns to me and says, "It's okay, happens a lot at this time in the morning. That's why I waited."

At the end of every day, the National Park Service workers collect and save everything that's left behind at the wall. There are warehouses full of the stuff. I don't think anything gets stolen from the wall. Even in a culture lacking a pervasive mythology, no one steals your suffering. The photos, letters, and mementos have special meaning to those who left them, and to those of us who choose to see them.

▲

2

HEROES

▲

T he primary task in the pursuit of salvation and healthy living
is to choose to respond to the summons of life's journey. The
truth is that you don't have to take somebody else's path or
identify with an established heroic figure. *You* are the principal
character in your own life's drama.

Our culture provides clues on which to base our journeys; so
do our families, communities, and religions. All of us have a unique
identity, something that binds us to our history. We also borrow
from other tribes to forge our own heroic paths. We can follow ex-
isting trails or create new ones. Growth and personal truth are
found on many paths.

I am writing this on the seventh day of Passover, when Jews re-
call the Exodus. At this time you are told to imagine that you per-
sonally escaped from the land of Egypt. Not your ancestors, not
some mythic voyagers, but you yourself. If you are to experience
personal liberation you have to make the journey yourself. You

▲

can't identify sufficiently with someone else's experience to confront the Pharaohs of your own enslavement.

The Hebrew word for Egypt is *Mitzrayim;* it comes from the root *tzar,* which means a narrow place. The Exodus is a story about the escape from a narrow place and it is a metaphor for the narrow places that all of us move through in our lives. We come into this world through a narrow place, squeezed, shaken, and battered, but we get through. For the next eighty years or so, we repeatedly come to places that seem too narrow, but we keep squeezing through. It is only by negotiating our way through the narrow places that we liberate ourselves from the constraints of our tunnel vision and become the heroic survivors of our own journeys. What keeps us stuck in the narrow places? Fear, pure and simple. We'd rather accept the certainty of the known than dare to imagine what might be on the outside.

Fear keeps us from making the journey. It keeps us stuck or sends us running off in any and every direction, instead of following the path of health and growth. The Coast Salish tribes of the Pacific Northwest tell this story about fear, which they personify as a double-headed snake monster named Sisquiutl.

The snake monster is sixty feet long and as big around as a giant redwood. At each end is a huge, swiveling head that enables it to see in every direction. Nothing falls outside its field of vision. If you come upon Sisquiutl, your instinctive reaction is to run.

But the Salish say the only way to escape the Fear monster is to stand still. If it sees you move, Sisquiutl will come after you, slowly moving first one end, then the other, until it traps you between

▲

both its heads. Then suddenly it sees itself and, horrified at its own reflection, slithers away.

The only way to deal with fear is to confront it directly—to stop and look at it. Then you can make it go away. Otherwise, you spend your life running from it and fear always runs at least as fast as you. When you let fear rule your decision-making, you're not choosing your own path. A Rwandan proverb says: You can outdistance that which is running after you, but not what is running inside you.

Most of us deal with the fear of making a new voyage by looking at a map and familiarizing ourselves with the landmarks so we know where we're going. Our lives, however, are not clear-cut paths to predetermined destinations. Things are always happening to us along the way. Our lives turn out to be a succession of surprises requiring mid-course corrections. We don't know anything about the end, only that it comes. If we stick to a plan without trying any of the byways, the end of the journey is just a place of preconception, not experience. Most of us have to know something before we do it, so we end up only doing those things that we've already experienced or that other people have told us are possible. That is not the heroic journey of life; it is a narrow journey with no surprises, no growth, no new experiences.

Life can't be mapped out in advance. Our journeys inevitably present us with things we can't understand—catastrophes, illnesses, traumas, losses, miracles, and ultimately death. Life is a journey of discovery, not certainty, and the best way to make it is simply to take it.

Since you can't know about your life before you live it, you just have to do it. If you have to know it before you do it, then you'll only do what you've already done. The heroic journey is in recognizing and confronting your fear so you can move past it to discover your truth. Where you are is probably where you ought to be. It's a place where you can learn something you probably need to know. Trust the process, not the plan.

The end of our journey is ultimately a result of faith, of believing that the journey is worth making. Before its end, we all experience lots of little leaps of faith. You can't know what will happen before you make the leap, because if you think about anything long enough you'll be immobilized by fear. Analytical thinking is based on preconception, but the learning that comes from experience is based on *living*. That kind of learning—about ourselves—is what makes us heroes. To make a leap of faith you have to be able to ask yourself one question: Is this what my heart tells me I need now?

I read about Bill Irwin in a newspaper article. He was a fifty-year-old recovering alcoholic who had lost his sight to an eye disease when he was twenty-eight. I don't know if his blindness and alcoholism were related, or which came first, but when he was almost fifty years old, he decided to stop drinking. During a quiet moment while camping with his son and grandson, Bill decided he would hike the entire 2,167-mile Appalachian Trail. He wanted this action to speak as a tribute to his faith—his faith in his son and grandson to see him through it, his faith in himself, and his faith in God.

Only 10 to 12 percent of all those who attempt it ever succeed

in hiking the entire trail. Bill's friends helped sponsor the under-
taking. An outdoor dealer in his Burlington, North Carolina, hometown donated equipment; individuals and church groups sent
contributions. In March 1990, Irwin, accompanied by his Seeing
Eye dog, Orient, left Springer Mountain, Georgia, on the way to
Mount Katahdin, Maine.

Orient sniffed out the trail and stopped at all the shelters. The
dog carried his own pack too, until it rubbed sores on his back.
Then Irwin carried that too.

There were a thousand steps that could have been fatal. There
were cliffs to fall over, marauding bears, blisters, despair, pain,
thirst, a broken rib, and blizzards. But Irwin said, "I don't care
how many times I fall; I can always crawl to Maine."

After eight months, Bill Irwin became the first blind man to
hike the entire Appalachian Trail. Friends, reporters, and well-
wishers joined him for the final 2.4-mile leg, but the last tenth of
a mile he wanted to walk alone, accompanied only by his guide
dog. As he approached the end of the trail, at the remote Katahdin
Stream campground, eighteen members of his hometown church
sang "Amazing Grace."

Blindness has nothing to do with physical seeing; it has to do
with believing. Bill never saw the trail, he just took it. He didn't
stick to the plan others preconceived was the life of a blind man.
He sought his own course, the one his spirit needed to follow.

It's an interesting paradox that the harder you try to "know it"
the less likely you are to "be it." Take the journey—it doesn't matter what you experience—only that you confront your reality.

I learned this painfully. Twenty years ago I had my first back operation for a slipped disk that sent such excruciating pain down my leg that I could no longer walk. First I tried an experimental procedure in which a cartilage-dissolving enzyme was injected into my back. I subsequently had three more operations. They failed to alleviate the pain and I was considering a fourth surgery. Then the surgeon and my mentor, Herbert Talaheftewa, told me to change my lifestyle and the pain would go away. The change meant no more competitive athletics, no pickup basketball games, no racquetball, no running or lifting weights. The pain was intense, but the likelihood of operative success was less than fifty-fifty.

So I decided to change my lifestyle. I began a program of daily traction, hot tubs, and swimming, and the pain actually lessened. My left leg was still shriveled and there was considerable sensory loss, but I began to feel better.

Encouraged by this diminution of pain, I began to think, "Maybe if I build up my musculature slowly I can resume my old athletic pursuits." I started by lifting my leg with a one-pound sandbag draped over my ankle. Then I gradually increased the weight to develop my leg muscles.

Every night while watching the evening news I followed this exercise program until I increased the weight to twenty pounds. I was feeling strong, infused with old confidence. I decided to make the final test of my success a rigorous climb up a steep mountain trail behind my house. If I could do that, it would indicate that I was ready to return to my old activities and could be a "real man" again.

I prepare for six months. On the appointed day, confidently clad in sweatsuit and headband, I launch the assault. I stumble and twist my ankles on the rock-strewn path. After two hundred yards, the pain begins. By a quarter of a mile, the pain is radiating down my leg. I keep walking, damned if after six months of work I will fall this short.

I'm not quite halfway up and I know I can't make it to the top. The pain is so intense that my foot begins to drag and tears obscure my vision. I cannot continue.

At the halfway mark is a flat ledge that overlooks the city. I've never stopped here before. I find a boulder and sit behind it. To my surprise an older man is already sitting there. Looking up at me, he sees my tears and dribbling nose, and asks if I am all right. Ashamed of my tearfulness, I wipe at my nose and say, "Yeah." He minds his own business and looks out over the lovely vista of the city below.

With tears still rolling I mutter, barely audibly (I think), "I can't make it to the top; I can't make it to the top." After a few moments, the man turns to me and says, "Maybe this is it." What does that mean? Maybe this is it, my walking days are over? Maybe this is it, I'm going to spend the rest of my life immobilized, a couch potato? Then it becomes clear: maybe this is it, maybe this is the top.

The top is where you can see farther than you've ever seen before, not some preconceived place where you think you have to be. If you have to be someplace other than where you are, you'll never see the here and now.

The fundamental problem that keeps us from staying healthy is

▲

that our bodies and our minds speak to us from two entirely different perspectives. Our heart, guts, backs, and legs tell us one thing, but our minds tell us another. The body understands and performs in ways that puzzle the rational mind. We continually ignore the body's messages by remaining fixed on only one certainty—what we know and think rather than what we feel.

The only way to see anew is to confront the reality of experience rather than always having to make sense of it. The world of experience—physical and emotional feelings—is not in opposition to the world of explanation; we just have to be willing to look at it again to appreciate both realities. Even if you've been dealt a terrible blow, the nature of the life force is movement toward equilibrium.

Dan was a beginning social worker when I first met him at a weekly training group I conducted at Maricopa County Hospital. Eager and bright, he was also severely spastic from cerebral palsy.

We lost touch with each other for many years until he came up to me after a lecture I'd delivered at the University of Arizona Medical Center, where he manages the Social Service Department. Dan said he'd like to write to me. Here's his letter:

> *When I first met you I was struggling with my cerebral palsy. I needed to be "supercrip," but my journey then was strewn with fear, anger, and sorrow. Over the past several years it finally dawned on me that I really could dance to my own music—that's what led me to the recovery of my spirit.*

▲

HEROES

In the old days, I cried for my losses in a voice that was so shaky it would never be lifted up in a church choir to sing glory to God.

I cried for loss of hands that so often I could not control. Hands that would never draw, paint, or create. Hands that gave me shame and that I desperately tried to conceal.

I cried for my legs that lacked grace. I walk like a goose or like a falling-down drunk. I cried for ballets I would never dance and mountains I would never climb.

Now what I hear is a voice that can soothe and heal. I touch people with my sounds because they feel my caring and I think now that God hears my labored song and welcomes it.

My hands? They still can't draw but they do create. They create a loving connection when I reach to touch someone in need.

As for my legs, sure they stumble and I fall, but grace I now treasure in a different way—I'm dancing through my life aware of my excitement in the journey and the adventure in every step.

I have still not totally accepted. I still hurt and cry, but awareness of my limits doesn't consume me anymore because I finally see that the real hurt is not what others inflict but what I do to myself. For not accepting the me that is, which is beautiful and still growing.

Why am I writing this to you? This is the next step you opened me to see. I accept with joy the truth that is me.

▲

I have lived for the last seven years with a partner who has AIDS. I'm gay (to date I've tested HIV-negative) and I'm also a recovering alcoholic. I'm comforted by declaring myself to you this way. It reaffirms what I've always known: If you're going to be it, own it. Thanks for the reminder,

Dan

Understanding our humanness with all of its strengths and frailties, fears and hopes, requires insights that may not square with simple causal explanation. Ultimately, it is in the experience of the journey that we heal ourselves, not in its analysis.

In the end, just as in the beginning, we can be, each of us, the heroes of an uncharted journey. We emerge from a contracting prison, squeezed, battered, deformed, gasping, bloodied, and screaming, "Here I am." It is in the journey outward, not in the safety of the womb, that we must emerge to fulfill our heroic possibilities. It is in passionate leaps of faith that we propel the human spirit forward. The safety of the known, which only leads to boredom, stifles the experience of life. As with heroes everywhere, the course of our lives may become a beacon to others who are on their own quests.

Make the journey. It doesn't matter what you experience, only how you confront the reality.

3

OLD PEARLS, NEW PEARLS

▲

The journey of heroes doesn't lead exactly to a predetermined end. But it's one to undertake, with all its uncertainties, because we know it's going to teach us something important along the way.

I like to travel by train; the hypnotic clacking of the wheels and the fleeting images in the windows go by faster than the days of my life. On the Amtrak from Philadelphia to New York, I saw in my trance the faces of old friends I would soon meet for lunch. Like the barren trees flashing by outside, their faces looked old and weathered too. There was a time when we saw each other daily; now years go by before we get together. I shuddered, and, roused from my reverie, told myself, "Lighten up. This is going to be a wonderful time."

I was sitting in the first passenger car behind the locomotive in the first row facing an empty seat. I took off my shoes and put my legs up. Not more than twenty minutes out of the station I was

▲

jolted from my reminiscences by the sound of the train's whistle. The multiple staccato blasts were followed by wheels screeching, then more blasts, lasting longer. I felt some bumpiness underneath my seat, then the train came to a halt.

After several minutes the conductor announced that the train was being unavoidably delayed; he didn't know why or for how long. A short while later he announced that we were awaiting the police and a coroner. Someone had lain down across the track and committed suicide. The bumpiness I had felt underneath me was the train running over the disarticulated remains of a human body.

My first response to all this was to look at my watch and wonder how late I was going to be for my long-awaited reunion. Maybe I'd get out of the train and walk to the next station. Then it came to me that somebody had just died beneath me, but I was already on to my next destination.

I like to see myself as warm and compassionately caring. So it embarrasses me to confront my self-indulgences, even in private. It's so easy for me to become desensitized to what's happening around me. Gandhi once said, "If you're going to be somewhere, be there," and I think these may be the watchwords for staying healthy. If you spend a lot of time being someplace other than where you are, it means the moment is never good enough.

There's a story about an old sage who, while walking down the cobblestone streets of his village, sees in the distance a young man approaching him. The boy's eyes are intently focused on the rocky path. Moving quickly and with great concentration, he sees nothing around him and inadvertently bumps into the old man. Startled, he looks up at the sage, who asks, "Where are you going, my son?" The young man replies, "I am going to catch my future."

The sage responds, "And how do you know you haven't already passed it?"

Your future has nothing to do with getting somewhere you think you need to be. It has to do with the awareness that getting *there* means being *here*.

Nobody was allowed to get off the train. We waited an hour and a half before getting under way. My long-awaited reunion was long over.

I checked into the hotel and then decided to go to the Rockefeller wing of New York's Metropolitan Museum of Art; it's one of my favorite places. It is filled with creations of spirit and passion that Michael Rockefeller, an anthropologist and collector, gathered before he disappeared on an expedition to New Guinea.

On a bench in a huge gallery I'm gazing at ornately carved canoes, each filled with detailed human figures that represent ancestral spirits being carried to the other world. Entranced by it, I wonder whether Michael didn't come to his end because he was a thief of their spirit. An old woman approaches me and says, "Excuse me, young man." To be considered "young" at age fifty immediately endears her to me. "Can you tell me what time it is?" she asks. Looking at my watch, I say, "It's exactly two o'clock."

She continues without hesitation, "I have a two o'clock appointment, and my friends were to meet me here but they have not yet arrived. It's not like me to be late. Frankly, I can't remember the last time I was. I came here today even though I have no interest in primitive art. Botany is my passion, I still work as a guide at the Bronx Botanical Garden. It's a voluntary thing. I just love flowers."

This is not a conversation; it's a monologue. She is speaking without comma or period. But as she goes on, it becomes clear to me that she has an appointment at two o'clock and I'm it! Without pause, she tells me she has recently endured a difficult time in her life. Her son died at the age of fifty-one. With tears welling she says, "There's something unnatural about parents surviving their children. I keep busy, though. I have friends, I go to museums, I plant flowers."

While she's talking, I look at her more carefully. She is wrinkled but is neatly dressed in a blue suit with a matching pillbox hat that's set just so on her head. In her white-gloved hands she carries a handbag on which are crocheted flowers. She is not more than five feet, two inches tall. While I am in this observational trance, I hear her say, "That's the secret of life."

I snap back to the moment. "Excuse me, what did you say?"

"I said that's the secret of life, sneakers are the secret of life." I look down and see that she's indeed wearing sneakers with her "Easter Sunday" ensemble. But what does it mean? I ask again, "Sneakers are the secret of life?"

"Yes," she says. "You can't wear them without moving. They're just not comfortable if you're standing still."

▲

At this point, an apologetic couple arrives, to whom she introduces me as the young man who has graciously been talking to her. I haven't said two sentences; she doesn't know my name. I ask her name and she says Pearl and then she's gone.

I've reflected on that bit of wisdom many times since. The secret of life is sneakers—you have to keep moving to stay comfortable.

Now I think that this is why the train was delayed; so I could come here and find this Pearl. Be where you are; don't always plan the destination; look at where you *are;* and keep on moving. That's the secret of life. The farmers say, "If you're green you grow, if you're ripe you rot." Same story.

I got delayed on the train and found the secret of life. See everything around you in this moment and then you'll see everything around you tomorrow.

I also think of Pearl's story in the language of science. Psychoneuroimmunology (PNI), a new area in medicine, emphasizes the idea that the body is an integrated circuit. The brain, the nervous system that guards against potential disease, and all other parts of the body and the mind are constantly communicating with each other.

The brain is not "the boss" firing commands to a captive audience. Rather, every cell in the body can send messages to all the others. Our enormously integrated circuits not only let cells communicate with each other, they can also recognize disease-producing strangers.

Every day, every hour, every minute, our bodies are invaded by

▲

viruses, bacteria, and toxins. They are in the air, water, soil, and the food that we eat. They live on tabletops and in coffee cups; they're exchanged in sneezes, coughs, and handshakes. Our own bodies carry them in every orifice, on our skin and in our internal organs. We produce cancer cells every day, but most of the time they don't kill us.

In spite of the omnipresence of these potentially life-threatening invaders, we generally thrive. The body resists disease because it is defended by the immune system, at the core of which are cells called lymphocytes. Each of us has about a trillion (ten to the twelfth power) of them and we have about a hundred million trillion (ten to the twentieth power) molecules called antibodies, which are produced by these lymphocytes.

Since you began this chapter, your body has produced ten million new lymphocytes and a million billion new antibody molecules. Each molecule is different and able to recognize potential invaders.

These lymphocytes and chemical messengers are transported through channels called lymphatics. The lymphatic system is a plumber's maze of tiny tubes that carry life-sustaining nourishment; it exists in addition to our circulatory system (the one that has arteries and veins and capillaries and whose life blood is pumped by the heart). The cellular warriors and chemical messengers of the lymphatic system, however, are not pumped by a heart, they are pumped by muscular movement.

Movement pumps the immune system! If you stop moving your body, if you just lie down and become inactive, you slow your immune response.

▲

Sneakers are the secret of life!

The old view that germs cause disease is an archaic myth. Germs don't cause disease! This doesn't mean that if you suffer from tuberculosis you don't carry the tubercle bacillus. But even if identical twins are exposed to a mother with TB who is showering both of them with the germs, one twin may get the disease while the other doesn't. Getting sick has at least as much to do with how you come to the germ emotionally as it does with how the germ physically comes to you. If, for example, you are depressed and miserable, you are more susceptible to getting sick. Depression inhibits the immune response, as does ongoing stress of any kind, which can include inadequate diet, substance abuse, other illnesses, work dissatisfaction, loss of a spouse/child/friend, and chronic fatigue. They all weaken the immune response as measured by decreased cell counts, biochemical assays, or lower activity of antibody cells.

The opposite is also true. We can enhance our immune response. Love, connections to things other than ourselves, things we believe in, Yoga, meditation, prayer, all can strengthen us. This wisdom is not new. Louis Pasteur, the microbiologist whose discoveries led to the pasteurization of milk, and Claude Bernard, a brilliant anatomist, discussed this idea more than a hundred years ago. Pasteur said it was the seed (germ) that made people sick and Bernard said it was the soil (people's bodies). On his deathbed Pasteur admitted: "Bernard is right, it's the soil."

We can measure immunoglobulins (an indication of immunologic strength) in the saliva of students. If we measure them before the students are shown a movie about Mother Teresa and

▲

again afterward, we find that the immunoglobulins go up. It doesn't matter what the student's sex or ethnicity or religious beliefs; just watching an evocation of love and caring strengthens their immune response.

At a recent meeting of the American Public Health Association, it was reported that a strong commitment to religious faith can promote health. This pattern held true for physical as well as emotional illness and for all religious faiths.

A recent report in the *Southern Medical Journal* suggests that after heart attacks people who were prayed for, even if they didn't know they were being prayed for, recovered better than people who weren't prayed for. Is it really possible that you don't even have to know, at a conscious level, that words, thoughts, and prayers are being uttered on your behalf in order for them to have impact?

The mind is an amazing tool. PNI scientists are finding out that the imagination can improve the responsiveness of the immune system as measured by increased lymphocyte production. Progressive relaxation through the use of guided imagery can increase natural-killer-cell activity in older people. Those are the cells that eliminate cancers. If you teach children with leukemia to imagine that the chemotherapy flowing into their veins is like the Pac-Man game they are playing and that one little gobbling Pac-Man creature is eating up cancer cells, those children do better than those who don't visualize.

Choice also strengthens the immune system. The mortality rate of old people in convalescent homes can be lowered by fifty percent if they are allowed to make even simple choices like what to have for their meals. In one study rats were injected with tumor cells. Some were then simply observed; others were placed in cages in which they were subjected to inescapable electric shocks, while others were placed in cages from which they could escape the shocks by jumping onto a little platform. The rats who learned that they could escape lived longer than the other two groups. Having choices and making our own decisions gives us more power to deal with whatever we have to confront.

I led a retreat for the St. Vincent's Hospital staff in Indianapolis, and we participated in a wonderful daylong workshop entitled Creating Healing Communities. In the afterglow of the closing banquet, two nuns asked me to join them at a place they thought I might like to see. I'd worked all day, we had just completed a four-course meal, the wine was freely flowing, and I'd sat through after-dinner speeches and awards, so I wasn't really enthusiastic. But it's hard to say no to nuns, so I went. Sitting knees to chest in their tiny car, I arrived at New Hope, a separate hospital-affiliated facility for the profoundly impaired.

Sister Francine motioned me to enter the sprawling 140-bed building from a side door so she could help a resident whose wheelchair was stuck in a soft shoulder. "How ya doing, Eddie?" she called and Eddie slowly said, "Reeeal goooood." Francine rolled him inside and as we continued down the hall she told me that he was the third sibling in a family to suffer from Friedreich's Ataxia, a disease of the nervous system that causes paralysis and affects speech. In the "old days" (about a decade ago) before genetic identification and testing were state-of-the-art, it was impossible to tell in advance who would get the disease, which only reveals itself in late childhood.

▲

These three siblings, now in their early twenties to mid-thirties, all lived at New Hope. Sister Francine stopped to hold each of them and each of the other residents we passed. She said hello to a severely retarded, hydrocephalic young woman who blew in Sister Francine's hair. Francine blew back. The patient held me and blew on me. Unselfconsciously, I blew back too. Francine greeted a young man who was profoundly impaired following a motorcycle accident, then another, a former rock musician, who silently moved his lips while tapping his head rhythmically, maybe to some imagined tune.

Sister Francine saw me shaking my head although I thought I was doing it imperceptibly. She said, "Whenever I go away, even for just a day, I see changes. Oh, they might be microscopic compared to the changes you see in ordinary people. When I see how they fight to keep moving compared to the ease with which I come to things, I know I've accomplished nothing in comparison.

"I look at what I start with and where I am. Then I look at them and how they've learned and moved, and it makes me humble." I thought: "She sees with eyes of joy and I look in horror and sadness."

"Come meet the Hoosier of the Year," she said and introduced me to John, a thirty-two-year-old man with severe cerebral palsy. He can't walk or speak clearly and has extremely limited functional use of his body. He has used a wheelchair since he was five years old. Next to him, also in a wheelchair, was Susan, his wife of two years, who also has cerebral palsy. Their wedding ceremony was attended by every resident in the New Hope facility, their families, and the whole St. Vincent's community.

▲

John was named Hoosier of the Year by the governor for his contributions to the Muscular Dystrophy Association. After John's closest friend at New Hope died of the disease, John decided to raise money for the organization. He got people to pledge pennies, nickels, and dimes for every mile that John would "run." How did he run those miles? The only way he knew how—backward, in his wheelchair. He has regular rhythmic control of his left foot only, so he moved inches at a time, pushing his wheelchair backward with his toes. He pushed himself through the streets of Indianapolis for hundreds of miles, raising more than $3,600 for research on muscular dystrophy.

John can't talk well, but he can move his finger across a custom-built alphabet board that fits onto his wheelchair like a tray. I sat on his bed watching him move one finger quickly, pointing out each letter in the words he wanted to communicate. He "told" me that one day while he was out on a road, away from New Hope, without the message board on his racing chair he was "found" by some people who thought he was running away. They wanted him to go back home. John became frantic, but, gesticulating uncontrollably in his desperate attempts to speak, he only frightened them more. In the two years it took him to raise the money for MDA, that was the only time he didn't complete his mileage for the day.

Then John told me he had cancer.

Sister Francine nodded her head. "Yes, it's true. A month ago John was diagnosed as having Hodgkin's disease." Hodgkin's is a cancer of the lymphatic system. I sat in disbelief. How much does a person have to deal with in one lifetime?

John had kept moving, but his biological limitations had am-

▲

bushed him again. He was not defeated, though. He intended to keep moving, through this new leg of his journey.

He pointed to his arm to show me where he got his chemotherapy. His crew cut, he said, was only partly from the barber. I asked him if he was going to complete this race, and with his rapid-fire forefinger he spelled out, "DOES A BEAR SHIT IN THE WOODS? If I can move I can win." Sister Francine smiled and told me he'd really cleaned up his language since he'd been married. Remember, winning is not necessarily curing; your spirit can be healed even if your body can't be.

Whether we tell the story anecdotally or scientifically, sneakers are the secret of life. If you can move you can win. The brain, the immune system, the nervous system, all of our hormones, are a constantly moving interconnected informational network. It isn't just the brain and what we know that control our destiny. Every cell in the body can communicate with every other cell as long as you keep them moving. It turns out that becoming and remaining healthy has far less to do with what we know than what we feel. What fuels the human spirit turns out to be closer to things like hope, belief, love, or faith than to intellectual certainty. The body feels the things of our spirits that our minds never thought of. Our cellular selves know things that are invisible to the eye. Trust your intuition. And keep moving.

▲

4
ON BULLSHIT

▲

I tried to find a different title for this chapter. My editor admonished, "If you can't say it on 'Good Morning, America,' don't write it." I said that anyone who had listened to the televised presidential debates in 1992 already recognized bullshit. Why not call it what it is? There's no other word for it.

Bullshit has become a prominent ritual in our culture. It's when people say things they don't mean; it's also when people mean things they don't say. The former is an active act of bullshit or bullshit by commission, if you will; the latter is more passive—we'll call it bullshit by omission.

Bullshit is the basic problem that keeps us from being emotionally healthy. Most of us pride ourselves on our ability to recognize it and therefore avoid being taken in by it, which is why we're so surprised when we become captivated by our own.

Let's try to be clear about what bullshit is and what it's not. It's not a lie; a lie is focused, it relates to a specific point. Bullshit is

▲

a whole program. A liar tells a falsehood to avoid the consequences of revealing the truth. Bullshitters, on the other hand, have far greater freedom. They are not limited to a particular falsehood about a specific point; they're prepared to fake an entire story, for a lifetime if necessary. Think about the former publisher of the *Arizona Republic* (Duke Tully) who, for over twenty years, perpetrated the hoax that he was a decorated Air Force fighter pilot. When finally confronted, he said he had done it because that's what he had always wanted to be. This kind of negative "creativity" gives rise to enormous opportunities for expansiveness, improvisation, imagination, and color—hence the notion of the bullshit artist.

What we say is often not what we believe and vice versa—and that goes for presidents, judges, NASA engineers, doctors, and religious leaders. All of the institutions that once sustained us have become less credible. We are being deluged by bullshit and growing so used to it that we choose not to see that the Emperor has no clothes. In public and private life, we've become more expert at denying what we really feel to be true than in acknowledging it. If we do it long enough it becomes difficult to distinguish what's real from what's make-believe. Then the BullShit becomes a Belief System and that's how we get into trouble.

In such an overwhelming barrage of stories told to make the teller look good, the search for truth easily gets lost. In a world obsessed with public relations and image, bullshit can run our lives.

So what is the truth? The truth is always closer to what we feel in our hearts than what we know in our heads. The body knows more than what the mind chooses to acknowledge. If you ignore what you feel long enough, it'll kill you. I'll tell you some stories about it.

Cherilyn was the only child of a genteel Southern family, raised politely in the fantasied culture of the antebellum South. Her father was an autocratic physician, her mother a demure, shy debutante. Her earliest recollection was screaming in terror in the dark. Her father always insisted that she "stop it," and told her, through her closed bedroom door, that there was nothing to be afraid of. If she continued to scream her parents left the house and instructed her nanny not to pick her up.

As she grew older she learned that all overt expressions of passion—whether fear, anger, or tenderness—were unacceptable. She could not get what she wanted by directly acknowledging her needs; only polite and reasoned discourse got her any attention. She grew up into a refined, controlled, and seething young woman. By the time she came to see me she was divorced from a man who had called her "the Ice Maiden."

Cherilyn developed intractable periodontal disease so severe that in spite of years of treatment her teeth loosened and were beginning to fall out. At age thirty-five, her teeth were so loose she could eat only puréed baby foods. Her illness could be seen as a symbolic need to be nurtured as she had never been as an infant.

The mouth is an interesting organ. It's the first we use after birth—we cry, we suck, we bite. It's the earliest instrument for expressing feelings. The child Cherilyn learned not to do any of them. Don't ask to have your needs met; you can't *ever* have what you want (which is different from you can't *always* have what you want); learn not to say what you feel. Once we've learned this or any other dysfunctional type of behavior, especially as a preverbal infant, it's hard to change, because there are always more reasons to maintain the old ways than there are to find new ways. For the Cherilyns of this world, growth has little to do with adding on; it has to do with letting go.

The body knows it's hurting, but the brain says, "Don't give up, be strong, don't cry, don't feel." To accomplish its ends, the brain produces a host of chemical messengers called stress hormones. They eat away at our immune systems, sooner or later breaking down our bodies. The body parts that become weak as a result are determined by a combination of genetics, organ sensitivity, and psychology.

Cherilyn needed to scream the truth of what she felt rather than pay attention only to what other people wanted. Unfortunately, too many of us become so tragically dominated by reason or the rules laid down by others that we lose our courage to feel. If we do that long enough, it makes us sick; there may be some psychological component in almost every ailment our bodies have.

Nobody fakes it till they make it; we fake it till we die.

Cherilyn was so terrified of expressing her truth with her mouth that she'd rot it out instead. She'd rather make herself ugly and smell bad than let it out.

When Cherilyn came to me, she'd been on antibiotics almost uninterruptedly for five years, to no avail. Nor did any amount of brushing, flossing, or gargling make any difference in her dental problems. That's because symptoms are just a way of expressing something we are unable to say any other way. If we could express our needs more truthfully, the symptoms would go away. But instead of looking for the truth about what the symptom represents, we almost always focus on the symptom itself. This is as foolish and useless as treating the fever of leukemia with aspirin and thinking we've cured the disease just because the fever disappears.

Cherilyn and I play a game. Every time she says "I think" I press an imaginary buzzer and make a flatulent noise, telling her to change it to "I feel."

I take her on imaginary voyages, some back to childhood. Imagination is not make-believe, it's the journey of an unfettered mind. When imagining her childhood she reexperiences the torturous events. This time, not thinking but feeling them, she cries, pleads, and rages.

I sing lullabies to her. The ceremonies of healing are not just in words; they are in music, song, smells, and movement; they are in objects and rituals.

Her gums improved and I didn't see her for a year, until she had a crisis in her business that triggered another gum infection.

She and her husband owned a small manufacturing company. Four months earlier, they had hired a new plant manager whom Cherilyn found intimidating. The new manager demanded that she come to him for any decisions affecting the plant, insisting that a consistent chain of command reinforced employee morale and efficiency. When a friend and valued customer called her directly one day and requested an urgent shipment, she ordered it. The following week the customer called to ask why his order hadn't

▲

arrived. She found the manager had intercepted her shipping order. He told her that even special requests must be handled
through established procedures because it was the only way to ensure quality control.

Cherilyn was livid and told her husband to fire the man. Her
husband agreed that the manager was inflexible and out of line
but also quite competent. If she couldn't live with him then *she*
would have to fire him and he would stand by her. But her husband didn't really believe she could do it. And she couldn't; within
three weeks her gums had again begun to ooze.

But even before she came to see me, Cherilyn dealt with the
problem herself. The manager walked into her office and asked
why her sliding door was open since it was summertime and it increased the air-conditioning bill. Cherilyn had had enough, and
she said, "Because I like the fresh air." In that moment, seeing
him retreat after she'd taken a stand, she knew she could face her
fear. Saying what she felt wouldn't kill her.

The limitation of psychotherapy is that talking about issues is
not enough. It's not enough to confront your truths in private. To
rid yourself of old, dysfunctional learning you have to slay your
dragons publicly. You cannot fulfill your dreams until you actually acknowledge them for others to see. Otherwise it's only your
head doing the talking without your body doing the walking.

Cherilyn decided to fire the man. She devised a termination ceremony and invited her husband, the shop foreman, her secretary,
and the bookkeeper.

With everybody present, she told the manager that this was a
ceremony of thanksgiving for her because she was ready to say

straight some things she had felt in her heart for the last year. "Your attitude, behavior, and way of speaking to me are unacceptable. You work for me, not vice versa. I'm giving you two weeks' severance pay. As of right now you are fired. Don't come back tomorrow." He didn't, and I haven't seen her since.

Symptoms are a way for your body to say "Listen to me talk for a change." This does not mean that every illness is cured when you clean up old beliefs. It means you can be healed even if you aren't cured. Healing is about paying attention to your damaged spirit, not only your broken body.

Gilbert was a fifty-year-old optometrist, the oldest son of an evangelical circuit-riding Tennessee preacher. He was trained from birth to follow in his father's footsteps. Gilbert had accompanied his father to the little Appalachian towns from the time he was four until his father's untimely death when he was fourteen. His father's death left an impoverished family who sustained themselves on the donations of parishioners and whatever work Gilbert did after school. He dealt with this burden outwardly uncomplaining but angry at God for not having provided the necessities that would have served as confirmation of his father's faith. For this anger, Gilbert felt shame and guilt. Such emotions are always crippling because they inhibit us from acting.

After completing high school, Gilbert was accepted on scholarship at a small Bible college. Its director had been a classmate of his father's who knew of the father's wish for his firstborn son to follow in his footsteps.

Gilbert knew by the end of his first year that he didn't want to be a minister. It was not his calling; instead, he wanted to pursue a career in sacred music at the college. When Gilbert told the director, he threatened to withdraw the scholarship. Gilbert studied what the director wished, and graduated, but he got even by never preaching. Instead he abandoned his religious vocation and became an optometrist.

I saw him after he developed chronic temporomandibular joint (TMJ) syndrome, a disease that can come from clenching the jaws tightly for many years. Gilbert's pain became so intense that it required tranquilizers, which only minimally lessened his pain. They also left him groggy and caused him to slur his words.

When he came to see me he was still angry at the Bible college director, at his father, and at God, and still crippled with fear and guilt. He couldn't express his anger, so he kept his mouth shut, actually tightly clenched to ensure no epithet might leak out. Of course, it was clenched so forcibly that he couldn't let his music out either.

After hearing Gilbert's story I suggested he go climb a mountain at dawn. When he reached the peak, I wanted him to scream every foul and vicious epithet he knew for three minutes.

His limited repertoire made it necessary for him to repeat himself over and over. Here he was watching the sun come up (and it's hard not to feel a sense of awe at such times), shouting obscenities and thinking about his father's certainty that daybreak was an affirmation of God's light and resurrected life. At first his angry words came out as just a peep. Then he *felt* his anger at God, at his father, at himself, and he screamed louder and louder until he wept. And then he discovered his jaws were open and that he was pain-free.

ON BULLSHIT

You can't sing praises until you confront your own rages, because bullshit steals your heart's song and that's where the spirit lives.

Gabrielle is an immigrant from Europe, who arrived in the United States after the Second World War at the age of seven. Her family experienced massive deprivation during the war, and her older sister always resented Gabrielle for having so many playthings after they left Europe. Gabrielle didn't want to feel good; how could she feel good when her sister suffered so? Gabrielle sought out pain; she became a social worker and dealt daily with pain. From age sixteen, she bled from chronic ulcerative colitis.

I was on her shopping list for a new therapist. After twenty years in treatment she was still looking for just the right person to cure her.

There is a part of me that enjoyed this. It fed my rescue fantasies: I'll succeed where others have failed.

Gabrielle already knew whatever I could teach her. She knew that suffering was her game and recognized it as bullshit; but from neurolinguistic training to macrobiotic diets and from psychoanalysis to surgery she'd tried it all, and still she bled. She saw it but felt blind when she looked for a way to react to it. She reminded me of Luke Skywalker fighting the robotic toy as Obiwan Kenobe tells him to just feel it, not to think about it. Otherwise, he'd always be a step behind. That is how Luke ultimately destroys the Death Star of Darth Vader—by trusting intuition, not knowledge.

But Gabrielle still wanted to know it, and I wanted to tell her that as long as she needed to know it she'd never see it. Psychotherapy is learning another way to see so that you don't reinforce your own blindness, but ultimately it's *you* who has to do the "seeing." The events in our lives aren't what stress us out; it's how we cope with these events that gets us in trouble.

Gabrielle participates in a four-day retreat that provides her with the context to look again.

On the edge of the Mogollon Rim, before a breathtaking vista, we are preparing to make rattles by wrapping plaster-impregnated gauze around small balloons.

First, the group is asked to visualize the balloon as the world, the whole universe. Imagine that as you fill it with your breath you are contributing your own life force to keeping it whole. Each of us participates in maintaining the balance of the world. As you bandage this planet, imagine you are healing it and yourself. Ultimately we will create an instrument that carries our life breath as a song. Give birth to your own healing music.

Gabrielle pursues the task to perfection. She blows up her balloon to just the right size, then wraps the plaster around it, waits until it hardens, cuts holes in both ends, removes the balloon and inserts the handle. Then she wraps it to anchor it tightly. Suddenly she remembers that she forgot to put in the pebbles. She has a solid rattle but one that makes no sound.

"Oh my God!" she says, "I forgot the pebbles." I tell her maybe that's the rattle she needs. She is crying and doesn't hear me. She wants a rattle that makes a sound.

"Make another one," I tell her. No! This is the one, so

▲

she unwraps it as fast as she can before it hardens. Through her tears and nose dribblings she pulls out the handle, inserts her pebbles, and rewraps it. But now, with the extra gauze, her rattle weighs about five pounds and looks like a mace. It is so thick and heavy that the pebbles make no sound at all.

She still has a rattle that makes no sound and suddenly she gets it: This is my song. I keep trying to find the right words while my instrument doesn't make music.

You'll never be able to dance unless you hear your own music.

It doesn't matter how you say it—the words on your lips must reflect the truth of your heart. Otherwise your life's breath is muted. When Gabrielle gets symptomatic now, she sings a song she wrote that says in part:

> Pain is a game
> to reinforce shame.
> It's not a history for which
> I am to blame.

Her outbreaks of severe colitis? Gone.

5

SELF-DECEPTIONS

▲

I pride myself in being an expert on recognizing bullshit. That's what I do for a living. I help people examine their self-deceptions.

You'd think I'd have learned enough by now not to be captivated by my own bullshit, but to some degree, it happens to me all the time. Without continued vigilance, I get complacent—that is, if you live with self-deceptions long enough, you become what you believe. The longer you've done it, lived it, learned it, the harder it hangs on, and the tougher it is to get rid of.

By the time we're three years old, many of the crucially important lessons in our lives have already been learned. One of the most basic and earliest things we learn is whom to trust. We learn early on that if we're hungry, somebody will feed us, or if we're hurting, somebody will pick us up and cuddle us (or we learn they won't). That's how we learn trust—by figuring out that either there is a nurturing, comforting, and sustaining world out there or that

▲

there isn't. Either way, once you've learned it, it's difficult to un-learn.

By early childhood we've learned something about the people who are important to us and whether or not we can depend on them. We learn to behave in ways that our parents and teachers want us to because we are afraid that if we don't, they will withdraw their love. Children conform their behavior to parental expectations because of the threat of the withdrawal of love. On the other hand, if children don't believe anybody really loves them, then it becomes very difficult to get them to conform their behavior to anybody's expectations, because you can't take away something from them that they already believe they don't have and can't get.

What we learned early in life about trust and expressing our needs shapes how we see everything that happens in our lives. We all operate on beliefs about the world that aren't really true . . . and it's hard to give them up.

Here are some of the things I learned, and even though I know some of them are garbage, they are hard to give up.

TRY HARDER! When I was in the third grade (over forty years ago), my art teacher said that if I couldn't "try harder" to keep my crayon lines inside the boundaries that I'd never be an artist. Until I began sculpturing at age thirty, and later even exhibited some of my work, I didn't believe I could ever be an artist.

BE CLEAN! This includes wearing clean underwear. My mother, like many, was afraid that if, God forbid, I should be run over on my way to school and brought bleeding and mutilated to an emergency room, the first thing the doctor would say is, "Did you see this kid's underwear? What kind of a family do you suppose he comes from?"

I've worked in a lot of emergency rooms and never once have I heard a physician say that. But I still wear clean underwear.

DON'T BE SELFISH! That means don't ask to have your needs met. Better to do for others what you'd like them to do for you than say straight out what you'd really like.

At a formal dinner party recently, I found myself looking at the one piece of pie left after dessert. I wanted another piece of pie, but instead of asking for it, I stared at it. The pie was practically looking back at me and winking. Finally I said, "Does anybody want that piece of pie?" Somebody at the table said yes and then asked, "Did you want it?" Of course I said, "Oh no," hoping he would think I was just asking for the pie because it couldn't speak for itself. "Don't be selfish"—I hear the old learning even though I know there's a difference between acknowledging my needs and being selfish. I still prefer for people to guess what I want. Then if I don't get it, I can always attribute it to their stupidity, which is a whole lot easier than dealing with rejection.

What else did I learn that still lingers? MAKE US PROUD OF YOU! KEEP IN CONTROL! BE STRONG! DON'T BE AFRAID!

"Don't be afraid" was a big one for me. Many members of my family did not escape from Nazi Germany. As much as I wanted to believe that I would not have walked to my death unresisting, I knew that I, too, would have been afraid and immobilized. I hated being afraid. My way of dealing with fearfulness was to make somebody else feel even more afraid.

I was afraid of the dark, so I tyrannized my sister, who was even more terrified of the dark than I was. On the streets of New York, near our tenement, I would tell her that monsters were coming out of the alleys and basements. She would clutch my hand and I would wriggle it free and run away from her. She'd scream in terror, which made my own fear more bearable and made me feel stronger.

These ideas can become Belief Systems. I still have trouble acknowledging my fear; I'd rather be angry. I've always nurtured an intense distrust for Germans. I believed that all Germans were tainted by the stain of the Holocaust—even those not old enough to remember it, which includes most Germans living today. It was as if some genetic encoding took place at the time of conception and anti-Semitism was somehow transmitted to succeeding generations.

When my parents arrived in the United States in the late 1930s, they spoke no English. Even though I was born in the States, German was my first language. Not too healthy for an American boy during World War II.

I never wanted to go to Germany and confront my Belief System. Instead I wanted to hold on to my rage. Then I came to Indian country, where I was judged to be just another white man. Nobody cared about my civil rights involvements or that I, too, came from a people once threatened with genocide. This was a new experience for me—I'd never before been just a generic "white man." I was always a New York man or maybe a Jewish man, and I resented being labeled that way or considered responsible for the atrocities committed against Indian people by earlier generations. That's when I became aware of how much easier it is to focus outward and judge others than to be on the receiving end of

▲

the judgment. To the Indians, I was just another "white man," so I was held responsible, just as I held all Germans responsible, even those Germans who were born after the war and who had no direct personal involvement in the actions of their fathers.

Holding on to anger makes us ugly, because it fills our souls with distrust that comes out in our work and in our relationships. Although I knew that my anger was a mask for fear, not until I was almost fifty years old could I go to Germany and face my fears.

My wife and I entered Germany by rail from the Belgian side; at the German border the conductors changed. In stark contrast to the disheveled Belgian, the German wore a crisp, starched uniform, and he was polite and formal. I was growing uncomfortable. The German landscape was clean, with no beer bottles, wastepaper, or accumulating garbage. I heard my mind's old, grim certainties whisper, "Clean! Efficient! Nazis!"

We got off in Cologne without a hotel reservation, and I plunged into the language of my childhood. I didn't want to like the place, but the mannerisms, the smells, the subtle formalities, seemed so familiar. It was the way I remembered my family, my neighborhood in New York: men bowing slightly when greeting; people addressing each other formally; napkins in napkin rings; the silverware placed just so; the coffee cups with thin lips; the pot roast black on the outside and soft on the inside. I thought: I love it and I don't want to!

The following day we took a boat trip down the Rhine. A loudspeaker on board played the lullabies of my childhood, and my tears welled up. In Frankfurt, we rented a car to go to my parents' hometown, a tiny village in central Prussia, a picture-postcard town built around a castle with the old Teutonic walls still standing. My family, on both sides, lived here for hundreds of years.

Prior to my arrival, my mother had written to an old family friend, a Gentile who is the sole repository of the Jewish history of this town and one of the few people still alive from prewar days. She told him I'd be coming with my wife and asked if he would please show us around.

As I drove into town I recognized the place from the stories and descriptions I heard in my childhood. This would have been my home, this farm town of only twelve hundred inhabitants of whom about a quarter were Jews and in which my ancestors had lived since the 1600s.

On the old cobblestone streets, I imagined my uncle's corpse being dragged after he was beaten to death on his doorstep by the Nazis. My heartbeat quickened as the old Belief System bubbled up.

I had lost the friend's address, so I went to a house whose number rang with familiarity. It was a three-story house with a quaint, ornate facade that had been converted into apartments. On each floor I knocked on a door; no answer. In the stairwells were tiny stalls, each containing a little toilet. Behind the house was a two-stall barn with cows.

I walked back onto the street and an elderly man hobbling with a cane approached me. In German he said, "You are Carl Hammerschlag," more a statement than a question. "You look just like your father." He hadn't seen my father in over fifty years, and it's true, I look just like my father. He introduced himself as Heinz, my parents' old friend. I told him I'd misplaced his address and he asked if I knew anything about the house I'd just entered. I said no, and he told me, "It's your father house." The first house I walked into in this town was my father's childhood home. I knew I was there to learn something.

Heinz invited us into his home and opened a bottle of wine and we talked. Even as I write this story I feel myself tingling. It was Friday afternoon, the eve of the Jewish Sabbath; this man was my mother's schoolmate; his older brother, Karl, was my father's closest friend. They both played fullback on the local soccer team.

We talked about family, mostly lighthearted banter. Then I told him I wanted to go to the cemetery before the sun went down. Jews do not go to cemeteries on the Sabbath when celebrations of life take precedence. Heinz had known I'd be going to the cemetery before I asked; he only wanted to know if I'd brought my skullcap.

The cemetery was half the size of a football field with fifteen rows of stones. I recognized every name. Everyone here was my relative. There were six gravestones with the Hammerschlag name. Heinz and my wife left me there, to be alone with my grandparents, aunts, uncles, relatives dating back centuries. Names from my childhood, names of families without survivors, names of the tortured. I recited the prayer for the dead, remembering the fears of my childhood and shuddering with the chill of still-stifled tears . . . DON'T CRY, BE STRONG, DON'T BE AFRAID . . . In darkness, I wept where no one could see.

Heinz took us, in silence, to his niece's home. She is the daughter of my father's closest friend, a non-Jew. She and I are exactly the same age; we would have been classmates.

I didn't want to be there; I wanted to wrap myself in my suffering. I had just returned from the pain of memory lane. No small talk. And she knew; she sensed that we had to speak in another way.

After the wine, she went into another room and returned with a letter. I stared at the yellowed envelope, recognizing the handwriting. It was a letter to her father from my father. She had saved this letter for fifty-one years, and I knew she had saved it for me. That was why I was in Germany.

She started to read the letter but the tears made it impossible for her to continue and she gave it to her twenty-six-year-old son to read. "My dear friend," my father began, "I write this letter from New York City. This is not the place of my birth nor the country in which I was raised but I am grateful to be here. My old homeland is a memory I will never return to. Still, I'd like to think that someday at least you and I will one day again be able to sit at the same table as the brothers we are."

My father saw what I would not allow myself to see. He knew that not all Germans were Nazis. He knew that nothing is so absolute that it cannot be seen again from another perspective. He had long ago come to peace with a struggle that has dominated my life.

For fear, I substituted anger and righteous judgment. Mine was the arrogance that came from certainty.

I knew she had saved this letter for me. As if reading my mind, she said, "The way you see us now is how we are and, I believe, the way we were." It was clear that she'd also kept the letter for herself and for her son. She was as much a survivor as I was. My father's letter to them is a family heirloom of forgiveness.

▲

I'm grateful to my father for helping me confront the old illusions. "I've got it now!" I thought.

We spent the night in the town's only hotel, which also happened to be the old town hall, but I couldn't sleep. I was awakened by screams. In my dream it was my persecuted relatives, but when I woke I heard the cat. At midnight I was standing at the window overlooking the old synagogue, which has housed several businesses during the last fifty years. Not a single one of them has been successful. I can see my relatives laughing; we're still here.

The following morning, Heinz picked us up early. He showed us the old Jewish houses in the village, told us who lived where, what happened in this house, where the ritual bath was, where the kosher slaughterer, the religious school. It was not just to me and Elaine he was telling this story; his nephew had joined us, and Heinz kept looking at him to be sure he noted the places and heard the names. He was telling this story to the boy as a legacy. This young man was to remember so he could tell the stories that would help us "sit at the same table." The boy listened carefully, took notes, drew pictures; soon he would become the storyteller.

I felt an enormous sense of gratitude and relief when I left the town. Our friends plied us with parting gifts, including a copy of my father's letter and sandwiches for the thirty-mile drive to Kassel, where we were to view the extravaganza called the "Documenta," an internationally renowned art and sculpture exhibit held every four years.

Outside the exhibition halls were craftspeople, portraitists, caricaturists, jugglers, and performers. I found myself in a group of about one hundred people standing in a semicircle watching a

young man on a unicycle. He was a talented juggler and come-
dian, and I was entranced by his performance and patter. He invited a little girl to sit on his shoulders and she caught the hoops
he juggled. Then he juggled fireclubs, then apples, from which he
took bites while he continued talking; it was a hilarious rap.

Getting off the unicycle, he picked up some grapefruits and juggled them with his palms down instead of up. While he was juggling in this unusual way, I heard him say, "If the Jews had learned
to catch this way then the whole history of civilization would have
been different." *(Wenn Juden es so gefangen hätten . . .)* I didn't
know what he meant, but the crowd laughed and I felt as if I'd been
stabbed through my heart.

My most feared fantasy had come true. That juggler's comment
proved to me that the ugly head of anti-Semitism *was* thinly veiled
beneath a veneer of civility—that it was present in all Germans,
no matter how young or old. I wanted to scream, "How can you still
be making fun of Jews?" but I could not speak because here, standing in a circle of a hundred Germans, I was afraid. If I opened my
mouth, they could drag me away. I was ashamed of my fearfulness.

At this moment my wife joined me and, seeing me ashen-faced,
asked, "Is something wrong?" Regaining my composure, I told
her that nothing was wrong. But the people who know you best
also know your evasions best so she asked me again. This time I
told her what happened. "I need to talk to him," I said.

After the performance he passed the hat around and then everybody left. I went up to him, daring to do it when we were alone,
and said to him in English, "I am an American" and he smiled
and said welcome. Then, I added in German, "But I am a Jew," to

which he responded, "It's a very sad part of our history." I glared at him, armed with indignant rage, thinking, now I've got you, you Nazi bastard. I demanded, "If it's such a sad part of your history how could you have said what you did?" Wide-eyed, he asked, "What did I say?" With clenched teeth I replied, "Don't tell me you don't know what you said." He looked at me, his mouth open, and again asked, "What did I say?"

I told him that when he was juggling the grapefruits upside down he said, *"Wenn Juden es so gefangen hätten*—if the Jews had learned to catch this way then all of history would have been altered." He said: *"Ich habe nicht Juden gesagt, Ich habe Newton gesagt*—I did not say *Juden,* I said *Newton."* I was standing almost thirty feet away and heard Juden, but he had said *Newton,* which in German, sounds almost exactly the same. He was talking about Sir Isaac Newton! If Sir Isaac Newton had learned how to catch palms down, the whole history of civilization would be different because he would never have discovered the laws of gravity! I didn't know whether to laugh or cry.

The way I heard it was not the way he said it. I heard what I wanted to hear, what I was primed to hear. What we hear has more to do with what we once learned than with what somebody has to say. I thought I'd just learned this lesson in my parents' hometown the day before. How many times did I have to learn it? How many times would it take to see? Every time you think you know something, look at it again and you'll know it differently.

I apologized and embraced the young juggler, who didn't know what to make of me, but assumed I came from Southern California. I was so happy. What would have happened had I not checked it out? What if I'd just done my usual thing and left, "knowing" that the way I heard it was the way he said it? I would have carried with me for the rest of my life the certainty that what I once believed had been corroborated by what I'd heard.

Yesterday I thought I had it. Now I really had it!

We continued our journey to Munich through a picturesque slice of Germany called the Romantic Road. Lush valleys, old castles, good beer, great pastry and sausages. In Munich some taverns still have singing waiters, and patrons, raising their steins high, join them in song. Of course, I imagined the Beer Hall Putsch and "heard" the Nazi songs, but I dropped it. I've got it now, I thought.

I saved one visit for last. Tomorrow I would go to Dachau, the Nazi concentration camp.

I arrived at Dachau early Monday morning so I'd have lots of time, time to look at every picture, to feel every reminder. Dachau was not primarily an extermination camp, but it had a crematorium. I was finally ready to witness the horrors for myself.

I approached the gate and saw a sign: "Dachau is closed on Mondays."

The irony of it; a Jew, locked out of Dachau. My whole life I had feared being in a concentration camp and now I was locked out. I walked around the perimeter. The camp was surrounded by a six-and-a-half-foot cinderblock cement wall with three rows of barbed wire on top. Standing on my toes, I could see over the wall. At one end was the administration building, now a museum. One barracks still stands; only the cement foundations remain of the others. There were no flowers, but the gravel walkways were raked clean.

▲

Then it became clear to me; Dachau was closed because I was not supposed to go inside. It was time to see Germany in a new way.

Every day for a week I'd confronted old expectations and certainties, and every day I had learned again what I needed to know. Every day offered a reminder—look again at everything you think you know.

6

CANCERS

▲

If our collective fund of knowledge is expanding as rapidly as the futurists tell us, then our old learning becomes obsolete before we know it. Using a computer-age analogy, since most of us have a limited capacity for incorporating new data into our previously programmed software, we go into intellectual gridlock and shut out new input. That's the same as digging in our heels and becoming increasingly certain that the way we see things is the only way there is.

Here is how old learning can kill us—kill our minds, our spirits, and our bodies.

Gerry was a forty-eight-year-old man whom I visited in the hospital after he was diagnosed with an inoperable cancer of the pancreas. Upon learning of his condition, he announced that he knew he was going to die and that he didn't want chemotherapy. His wife, a nurse, became angry with him because of his resignation. She wanted to make him into an exceptional cancer patient, one who

▲

fights the disease and says: "It doesn't have me, I've got it, and I'll do whatever it takes to live fully, now."

In his heart, though, Gerry "knew" *it* had *him*. The cancer was the final acknowledgment of his destiny. He told me he was "just like" his mother, who had died at forty-eight of an inoperable gastrointestinal cancer. "What do you mean, just like your mother?" I asked. "Well, my three brothers were football players and mechanically inclined outdoorsmen 'just like' my father," he said. Gerry, on the other hand, was artistic, bookish, and introverted "just like" his mother. Everybody commented on the similarity of their natures. She died an agonizingly slow death, which Gerry witnessed. Her final words to him were, "Take care of yourself, son," which, in his unconscious mind, he heard as, "You're going to die just like I did." From that moment on, he knew he too would get sick.

All his life he believed he would die the way his mother had. And within six months of his initial diagnosis, he was dead of the same disease that killed her. Talk about programmed software. The truth is that he wasn't just like his mother and he wasn't destined to die like her. That was a misinterpretation of the message; just because you are *like* someone doesn't mean you *are* that person. You may have a genetic predisposition for certain organ weaknesses, but that doesn't mean you are programmed to deal with that awareness by rolling over and dying. Whatever "it" is (cancer, some other catastrophic illness, or a hurdle in your life), how *you* come to *it* is at least as important as how *it* comes to *you*.

If you come to it believing you are powerless to alter some preordained decree, then it's got you. If, on the other hand, you dare to believe that maybe you can alter the decree, maybe through some awakening you can find new learning, some new awareness, perhaps even experience some joy. If you believe that, then you've got it—then at least healing, if not curing, is possible. Gerry's belief, as much as his disease, caused him to die the way he'd always believed he would.

Researchers have now shown that prayer, a sense of personal power, love for pets, a family—all promote a healing response.

As an eight-year-old, Susan had watched her grandmother die of breast cancer. Thirty years ago, when treatment options were significantly fewer, her grandmother had received radiation treatment, which caused skin ulcerations that never healed. Her breast became an oozing, foul-smelling, festering sore. Susan could only visit her grandmother after the room was sprayed with a deodorant; otherwise, the odor made her sick to her stomach.

The last thing she overheard before her grandmother's death was a conversation between her mother and the doctor. Susan's mother asked whether the disease was hereditary. The doctor replied, "It usually skips one generation."

From the time she was eight years old Susan "knew" that she would die from cancer of the breast.

At age thirty-five she had a breast malignancy diagnosed, and Susan elected not to have surgery or radiation. In spite of the magnificent advances in treating this disease in recent years, she believed that megavitamins, a nutritious diet, and prayer were her only answers. She also believed, with certainty, that her grandmother's fate would befall her if she was treated by doctors. She didn't trust them, so she never looked for one that she could feel different about. She decided all doctors were the same, and the result of this decision was that she died of metastatic disease within two years. Susan had preprogrammed her software and never updated it.

Paul is a thirty-three-year-old computer genius whose neck is scarred and misshapen by a skin grafting to conceal a massive cavity, the result of surgical removal of a malignant cancer of the nasopharynx.

The youngest son of a frequently absent father, Paul was often awakened as a child by his mother to go on midnight searches for his wayward Dad. From the earliest age, she told Paul how he was the only one she could trust, how his father and his older brother were undependable and uncaring. Paul was her "special boy," he would not let her down, and she would always be there for him.

Every young boy dreams of a special relationship with his mother. In this case, however, Paul really did have her all to himself, but the closeness came with a price. She expected him *always* to be there for her and with her.

Paul worked while going to school to put money away to buy his mother a house. He won a full-tuition scholarship to college, studied day and night, and rarely dated. When he entered graduate school at age twenty-one, he fell in love with the cashier in the express cash-only line at his local supermarket. After six weeks, he proposed.

She was an abused, chronically depressed eighteen-year-old who wanted to escape her alcoholic father, so she married Paul. He loved her neediness and promised he would "always be there" for her. Programmed software.

▲

CANCERS

He enrolled her in a community college while he worked on his doctoral degree. She had no interest in school but he wanted her to improve herself. She didn't like going to class, so he attended in her place, did her assignments, and took her exams. She got the degree.

After the wedding, she never worked again. They had three children, and she had chronic migraines and severe bouts of recurrent depression. Whatever he did was never enough to help.

When he wanted to give up and run away from it all, Paul went back to his mother's house in his hometown. His mother indulged him, but his wife complained that he wasn't available to her, so he always returned sooner than he wanted to. For a decade, he dreamed of leaving, but of course he couldn't, because she and the children needed him.

That's when Paul developed an invasive cancer in his sinuses, which, as fate would have it, turned out to be best treated at the medical center in his hometown. Paul got a cancer which involved escaping from his wife and being cared for by his mother.

Paul chose to deal with his programming differently than Gerry and Susan did. After we worked together for some time, he learned to say no and even to ask directly to have some of his needs met. Instead of doing for others what he really wanted for himself, he acknowledged his needs and filled them more directly.

Paul is a long-term survivor. How you feel about what you've got is at least as important as what you know about it.

Do the examples of Gerry, Susan, and Paul tell us that we can program our bodies? Research findings in psychoneuroimmunology now provide hard data that suggest this is possible.

▲

In each and every one of us, cancer is always happening. We grow cancer cells every day. But the cells of the immune system, which is responsible for recognizing invaders, identifies these outsiders and destroys them. We can promote the immune response if we come to illness from inner strength, faith in ourselves, and connections to others. Those factors can help determine the course of disease.

A number of rats were injected with tumor cells, and given the same diet, living conditions, and treatment. But their survival rates varied widely. When the data were carefully analyzed, the scientists discovered that the rats which died first were housed on the topmost shelf of the cage room, while the rats that survived the longest were from the lower shelf. The only variable that wasn't controlled was that the lab assistant who fed the animals was too short to reach the higher cages, so he hand fed and touched only those rats he could easily reach. He fed the others by placing feeding bowls in their cages but not handling them at all. Being touched, held, cuddled, and "loved" promotes the healing response, even in rats.

Making connections is what healers ought to be doing: listening to people's stories, finding out how we can best be with them as they face their disease.

A young woman named Maria called my office one day saying, "I have to see you. I heard your name over a year ago and then yesterday, in a dream, your name came to me." My initial, if unspoken, judgmental response was: "Give me a break—not another channeled intergalactic traveler!"

But if I come to someone in a dream I like to find out why. On

▲

her first visit, Maria said she'd dreamed of a patriarch and his face was mine. She'd never seen me before. And then she saw an image of coiled snakes, but they did not strike. She hated snakes, but this time she spoke to them, saying: "Uncoil and save yourself."

I have a sculpture of a coiled rattlesnake on my wall. As a matter of fact, it hangs right in the midst of my diplomas. It's my special animal, one that reminds me not to take myself too seriously. When Maria saw the sculpture, she said, "Now I know why I am here." I didn't know then that the reason she came was to teach me how to connect with those who seek my healing in ways I never imagined.

A year earlier, doctors had discovered Maria had a slow-growing colon cancer. This disease is curable with surgery, but Maria refused and chose a course of radiation therapy. After nine months, the radiation hadn't helped and doctors found that the tumor had spread. Surgery was again recommended, but now a colostomy was necessary, an opening from the colon through her abdomen draining into a collection bag. Maria refused, deciding instead to follow a strict macrobiotic diet. Her surgeon said he couldn't participate in that decision and she should find another doctor. She found me.

Maria had refused surgery as the result of a dream. She dreamed she was having her house renovated with a new door made in her bedroom that opened out into a flowering garden. The flowers beckoned to her and she wanted to walk out, but the door wouldn't open. Terrified, she grabbed the doorknob and pulled at it, bracing her feet against the wall, but it wouldn't budge. Maria took the dream to mean she shouldn't have surgery. What did I think? I said maybe the dream was about learning to find other ways of getting out.

She never did undergo surgery, but what happened in those last six months forever changed the way I practice medicine.

First, she confronted and expressed her rage at the doctors who gave up on her. Then she dealt with her anger at herself for not initially deciding to have surgery. Maria didn't want me to save her. She wanted me to listen to her and be with her on the journey.

Maria was fascinated with things Native American. Sometime, long before, she had even taken an Indian name. She asked me if I could arrange a healing ceremony for her. This was the one thing she wanted to do for herself in whatever time she had remaining.

Three months after our meeting, she had an emergency colostomy for an obstructed bowel, during which it was discovered that half her liver had also been invaded by tumor. She had become so emaciated that what little flesh she had on her bones was breaking down over all the bony prominences.

She was receiving over 200 milligrams of morphine daily in a continuous IV infusion for the intense pain. She had already visited a lawyer to settle her affairs and decided to be cremated. She wanted this ceremony as a final transition.

It's not the kind of thing I do for my patients, but I felt that after almost a year together, I could not abandon her. Furthermore, here I was challenging her to confront herself truthfully, while I waffled about the propriety of asking my Indian "relatives" to do a ceremony for her.

I asked and a Native American church spiritual leader agreed to her request, so we planned the all-night ceremony. Maria was

▲

ecstatic; though she was dying, she felt energized. She invited all the important people in her life to come, as directed by the Native American church "Roadman." She invited her children, companion, and friends. This was to be her legacy to us.

The meeting was conducted in her friend's family room. In the middle of the floor rested a four-by-four-foot wooden box about three feet deep, filled with sand. Howard, Maria's family physician and an amateur cabinetmaker, had built it for her ceremony at her request. He said it was the first time he'd ever participated in a terminal patient's last wish.

In the box filled with sand, a small fire burns, surrounded by a half-moon-shaped earthen altar. This ceremony, usually conducted in a tipi, takes place right in the middle of the city.

More than thirty people sit in a circle around the box. The Native spiritual leader asks Maria why she asked for this meeting. She says this ceremony is the fulfillment of a dream. She's always wanted to be part of the healing of the earth, to see her life as a vehicle for others to discover the world as one family with one spirit. "I want my children here to remember me this way, not in pain but in hope." She turns from the fire to the Roadman and says, "I want you to help me on my journey."

Then the drumming and chanting and all-night prayers begin. Everybody who wants to has a chance to speak. Sometimes Maria sits up, sometimes she lies down, sometimes she moans in pain.

Can you imagine the important people in your life coming together for you? Everybody says something, as much for ourselves and each other as for Maria. People speak about what they want to do with their lives, about Maria's influence on them, even now, maybe especially now.

When it's her turn, Maria says this ceremony is the culmination of her life. "I have dreamt about this since I was a child. You make my dream come true."

With the IV bottle and plastic tubing dangling from her bathrobe, she shuffles to where her children are. Looking at them she says, "When you remember me, picture me like this, smiling and with my spirit soaring." Her tears (and mine) are the tears of love.

The medicine man blesses her, waving an eagle feather fan over her and brushing the cedar smoke over her whole body. Then, touching her, he says, "Thank you for sharing your life with me."

That's how I want to go, surrounded by people who love me, thanking me for being part of their lives.

Maria actually lived for another couple of weeks. Days before her death she gave me a small snake she'd made out of Play-Doh. "Here is your special animal," she said. Attached to it is a little card saying, "I'm always there when you knead me."

I carry it in my medicine box. It reminds me how I'd most like to be as healer and as one being healed.

7
BELIEVING IS SEEING

▲

Can you remember the first time your dreams came true?
For me, it was when I was seven years old and obsessed
with playing a game called Gyp Joint on the streets of New
York. You cut a little square door out of the edge of a cardboard
carton and then turned it upside down on the sidewalk. You invited all comers to try to shoot a bottlecap from the curb through
the door and into the box, a distance of about fifteen feet. If it went
through, you paid the shooter five caps, maybe ten, depending on
the size of the door opening. If they missed, you kept their cap. If
the door was just about the same size as the cap, the odds of flick-
ing it through from that distance were astronomically small and
odds of 50 to 1 were not unheard of. This is how I learned math.

I'd fill my caps with wax to give them more weight and stabil-
ity. Once I shot a cap through a door so small the payoff was an
incredible 60 to 1. Kenny Kimmelman couldn't believe I'd shot it
through. It took him a month to pay me off and then my mother

▲

wouldn't let me keep "that garbage" in the house; but I knew that dreams can come true.

When I was eleven, my beloved New York Giants were in the National League pennant race. It was the last game, and the Giants were down by three runs in the bottom of the ninth inning, with two men out and two men on base. Bobby Thompson faced Ralph Branca of the redoubtable Brooklyn Dodgers. I had cut school, my ear was glued to the radio, fingers crossed and lips pleading, "God, let him hit a home run." And Bobby Thompson hit a 3–1 pitch barely over the left field wall and I knew dreams can come true.

The Giants never won a World Series, though, until 1954. In the opening game, my idol, number 24, Willie Mays, raced after a ball hit by Vic Wertz of the Cleveland Indians that took off like a cannon shot. It was uncatchable, another tragic portent for this series, but Willie started after the ball. Even though I knew he'd *never* catch it, I still prayed, "Let him catch it," and he did! He caught the five-hundred-foot drive over his left shoulder and then, more miraculously, turned to unleash a throw that held the other runners on base. It was that catch and throw that turned the series around. I knew the power of prayer and not to say "never" again—dreams do come true.

I loved baseball and played it in high school. Now I don't even watch games on TV. Haven't been to a ballpark in twenty years. I do go to baseball movies, though. Buy lots of popcorn and sit through the show stuffing my face. It's not quite like watching Hurling Harry, the legendary Polo Grounds peanut vendor who could accurately throw a bag of peanuts thirty feet overhanded, under-

THE TALBOT BANK

P.O. Box 949 • Easton, MD 21601-0949

ACCOUNT 050140 1806

DATE Sept 13, 2001

NAME Dr. Keith Coleman

CHECKS AND OTHER ITEMS ARE ACCEPTED SUBJECT TO VERIFICATION AND COLLECTION AND UNDER THE PROVISIONS OF THE UNIFORM COMMERCIAL CODE AND THE RULES AND REGULATIONS OF THIS BANK.

DEPOSITS MAY NOT BE AVAILABLE FOR IMMEDIATE WITHDRAWAL.

ALL CHECKS SHOULD BE ENDORSED WITH YOUR NAME AND CODE NUMBER.

CASH		
CHECKS (LIST SEPARATELY)		DOLLARS
		60
		60
		30
		30
		—
TOTAL ITEMS		
TOTAL ►		180

CHECKING DEPOSIT   131 TALBT 005-00041
6 0 13-SEP-01   09:12   050140 1806
180.00

Thanks for Banking With Us

handed, hook shot, under his leg, right into your outstretched hands. But the memories are all there.

When I saw *Field of Dreams,* I was reminded of my old dreams and how long it had been since I truly believed they could come true. The movie is about a man whose father had nurtured his own unfulfilled dreams through the son's baseball skills. But the son shunned the father, who died before the boy could make amends. My inner psychiatrist voice says, "Here is a wound that never healed."

In the story, the son, Ray, a struggling farmer, builds a baseball diamond in his cornfield—knowing it will jeopardize his crop—after hearing a voice that whispers, "If you build it he will come." And sure enough, he builds the baseball diamond and it's visited by Shoeless Joe Jackson and the rest of the disgraced 1919 Chicago Black Sox. Other players come too, players whose dreams were also dashed, and then, at the end, Ray's dad shows up as the young ball player Ray never knew. When his father invites him to play catch, he grabs this last chance to heal the wound. I cried when I watched this movie; fortunately, the theater was still dark so nobody could see me dealing with my own unfinished business with my father.

All of us have unfulfilled dreams, wounds that need to be healed, old business that seeks resolution. We simply don't create the "field of dreams" necessary to allow that to happen. It's not because we don't want to, it's because we don't believe.

I had a much easier time believing when I was a kid. Dreams and miracles were ordinary because then I understood that "believing is seeing." I had not yet grown up to learn that only "seeing is believing." I wasn't yet jaded by skepticism, life experience, and losses. When my little-kid dreams didn't come true it was just for that day, it didn't mean that tomorrow was tainted by yesterday's failure. Every dream, every possibility, was an independent event and no previous testimony could ever color today's possibilities. Nothing shook my faith.

I got older. I experienced failure, saw my hopes dashed, watched my doubt and cynicism grow, until one day I only saw the way it was, not the way it might be. This is the ultimate blindness. This kind of blindness has nothing to do with sight; it has to do with lack of vision, and vision is the stuff of dreams, hope, and possibilities. Most of us scale down our dreams to the size of our fears until our vision becomes so tunneled we see darkness everywhere.

Here's how I learned to see in the dark—with Mona's help.

I call Mona my sister and the word truly describes how I feel about her. She is a wonderful Native American healing woman who has helped teach me how to pray. Facing a career change, she invited a Sioux medicine man to conduct a Yuwipi ceremony for her. I'd heard about the ceremony for years, but had never participated in one.

This ceremony, one of the sacred healing rituals of the Sioux, takes place at night. The medicine man, known as the Yuwipi, calls the Spirits into the gathering in the pitch dark. The Spirits reveal their presence in flitting lights like tiny flashes of lightning, in shaking deerskin rattles, or in the sound of beating wings. They only come in absolute darkness, and sometimes they take your breath away.

In the old days, the Yuwipi man would be bound with rawhide

laced from his fingers to his feet and then wrapped, like a mummy, in a blanket and laid down in the center of this circle of darkness. He would free himself from his ties by calling upon Spirit helpers who, in helping free him, would also help free the other participants from whatever bonds chained them. Nowadays the ritual varies a bit, but the elements are still the same.

The medicine man came down from South Dakota, a two-day drive if you take few breaks. He charged no prearranged fee, although Mona and her family promised to make a contribution. He came because he was called upon and therefore felt obligated to do so. I may go down the block to see a patient, but to travel across the country? That's commitment to your calling.

No traditional Indian healer I know ever asked to become one. Unlike modern medical practitioners, they didn't choose their vocation, it chose them. They accepted, often with great reluctance, because they knew it wouldn't be easy; your life is no longer your own.

The meeting is scheduled for nightfall. The Yuwipi man doesn't arrive until midnight. He introduces himself, his wife, and a helper. He speaks with Mona alone in the kitchen, asking her about the need for the ceremony, her prayers, her dreams, what's happening in her life. When the consultation is over, he comes into the living room, which has been cleared of furniture. About thirty people are gathered in the fourteen-by-twenty-foot space. All the windows are covered. Most of us are sitting cross-legged on the floor around the periphery, a few on the only re-

▲

maining sofa. He instructs us to take off all our jewelry, watchbands, eyeglasses, anything that can possibly reflect light. He says that the Spirits love the darkness and, "If you don't respect them they'll yank things off of you, they'll pick you up and turn you around."

He asks for the lights to be turned off to see if there are any cracks of light from the outside. When one appears through the door frame he stuffs towels into it until the room is completely sealed, totally black. He puts the lights back on and places a blanket in the center of the room. This will become his altar.

Mona and her sisters have spent days making a string of hundreds of tiny tobacco ties. They made little bundles by wrapping tobacco in pieces of cloth, each about an inch square. The colors of the cloth—red, black, yellow, and white—are the colors of the four directions, and the bundles represent all the peoples and directions of the earth. They are no bigger than the size of a raisin and are attached to a string at intervals of about an inch apart, until they stretch for what seems a mile. It has taken Mona many days to prepare this. The Yuwipi man takes the tobacco tie string and winds it around the edges of the blanket. Now it becomes sacred space, it separates him from us and connects him to the Spirits. But there is not more than sixteen inches between our feet and the altar.

On each corner of the altar he places a large tin can filled with sand, into which he plunges a wooden staff. With its distinct color, each staff represents one of the car-

dinal directions and onto each are tied four larger tobacco
bundles, one of each color. Between the red and the black
staffs is another tin can into which he puts five staffs, all
of which have red tobacco ties. There's an eagle feather on
the central one; he says it represents the power and wisdom
that comes from above. At the base of this can is a paper
plate filled with fresh raw liver. In the old days, he says, it
would have been freshly slaughtered dog meat. Into his
sacred place he brings eagle feathers, his sacred pipe, then
Mona's pipe and those of others, and then the rattles. They're
made of deer hide and inside are tiny pebbles called Yuwipi
stones. He says he gathers them from tiny anthills; they
make the music the Spirits hear and will also speak to you.

This is a Spirit-calling ceremony. If you believe Spirits
will come, they may caress you or confront you in ways you
can't even imagine, like with an ecstatic vision.

He fills the pipes with tobacco while his helper sings the
appropriate pipe songs. He holds each pipe up, prays with
it, caresses it, and then places it lovingly on his altar. After the pipes are loaded, his helper comes around to each
of us and gives us a sprig of sage, which we are to put behind one ear; this will help bring the Spirit to us. Then he
comes around with a tin can filled with coals onto which
he puts sage; he then brushes the smoke onto us with an
eagle feather to cleanse us and the room. We are sanctify-
ing the space, purifying it for the coming of the Spirits.

Standing in the middle of his altar, the Yuwipi man says
we are about to begin and that we should not be afraid.

Each of us will have a chance to express ourselves when we hold the sacred pipe that he'll pass around. Say whatever you want, he tells us, say why you're here and what you want.

The lights are extinguished. The darkness is so intense that there is no adjusting to it. The only other time I've experienced such blackness was in a cave a mile beneath the earth's surface. In the darkness everything becomes magnified, every sound, every breath. The feathers sound like the beating of wings, a baby's cry penetrates someplace deep inside. I can feel the leg muscles of the person next to me tightening. This visual deprivation makes my mind race. I'm trying to concentrate so I can gain some control over these feelings of isolation.

The drumming and songs begin. The Yuwipi man begs the Spirits of the four directions to honor us by their presence. I hear flapping wings. The rattle is so clear I can distinguish each tiny pebble as it moves within. Then I see tiny lights flashing. My mind says it's some kind of fiberoptic strobe, but whatever the light is, it doesn't illuminate anything. I hear the rattle sound coming closer.

Without warning I feel something hit me between the eyes. My shock is so profound it snaps my head back and I bang against the living room wall. Then the rattle moves away. Did "he" hit me with a rattle? How come it was so soft? How did he find my head and how did he stick it right between my eyes? How can he see me when I can't see him? How come he can move around in that narrow space with-

out stepping on my toes? Was it him? Are there Spirits? What do I believe? What do I see?

The message becomes clearer to me. I think I see, but I am blind. I have sight but no vision. My questions keep me from being by always focusing on knowing. The Yuwipi man's Spirit knows I'm always looking but not always seeing. What's the difference between sight and vision? Vision is the capacity to believe in what my heart sees, what others can't see. Vision is seeing positive possibilities where others see only negative probabilities.

The Spirit's thump on my head helps me see that I seek to be a visionary, yet guard against it by making current realities fit old experience. If you have to be sure about what you're experiencing in the moment you'll always subordinate the reality of the present to the certainties of the past. The blow between my eyes is a reminder that a visionary is the one who learns to see in the dark, not the one who describes it.

The next time the rattles come I'm leaning back, and still they find me. But this time they caress my face and move on. Something knows I've seen something. By the time the pipe comes to me I can't talk, my lips won't move. What a wonderful teaching! You don't have to say it, explain it, or understand it to know it, you just have to feel it. Mi takuye oyacin is all I say—to all my relations— thank you.

After each person has had the opportunity to express himself or herself there is a closing prayer and concluding songs. The lights come on, the pipes are lit and passed around, and then we share a festive meal.

When the lights come on I see that the raw liver is gone. Each of the corner poles that held the four different-colored tobacco ties now holds only the tobacco bundles of its own color. How did he do that in the dark?

Of all the people in the ceremony I was the only one who got smacked between the eyes. How did they/he/it know what I needed to see? Don't know, don't care.

All around us, there are those who can see in the dark.

I participated in a weeklong Jewish spiritual retreat not long ago. During a small group session, a grotesquely spastic cerebral palsied man shuffled his way toward us. I hoped he would pass us by and go elsewhere so I wouldn't have to look at him, knowing full well I'd be riveted by the writhing, snakelike movements of his head and extremities.

Of course, he joined our group and attempted to introduce himself. His speech was unintelligible and required so much attention that I found myself unconsciously forming his words with my lips and tongue to ease my sense of his suffering, which was, of course, only my suffering.

When it was my turn to introduce myself to the group, I was looking at someone else until the palsied man commanded my attention by his inarticulate garbling and waving. I looked at him and he pointed to his lips and I struggled to hear him say, "I want to see your lips, I hear with my eyes." In addition to being palsied, he was deaf too! I had to look at him.

The following day was the Sabbath celebration, the highlight of the week. As I entered the hall, to my amazement, I saw the same man sitting on the stage. The entire four-hundred-member gathering was going to listen to him deliver the commentary on the week's Torah portion. He approached the lectern with an interpreter, and when I looked at him, I saw his arms jerking, his face grimacing, his voice beyond understanding. But when I listened to the interpreter translate his story I suddenly saw him dancing and singing, his voice a love song as he told us how he was gifted by God to be able to speak without a tongue, to listen with his eyes, and to dance without the grace of movement.

He sees in the dark.

Here's another who does.

As an eighteen-year-old, Hugh was already considered one of the best competitive rock climbers in the country. Caught in a blinding blizzard while on a climbing expedition, he strayed from his intended route and crossed a snow-covered stream, breaking through the ice into the water below. His feet were soaked and rapidly freezing; blinded by snow and exhausted, he built a rudimentary shelter. After two days, rescuers found him under a spruce-bough lean-to, nearly dead from hypothermia and severe frostbite. Both his legs had to be amputated just below the knees.

Five weeks after the amputations, with new artificial legs, Hugh climbed a steep trail near his home. Within a year, he'd learned to design and make himself new feet. For walking, he screwed in a fairly flexible, natural-shaped foot. He created feet for specific climbing conditions. For most climbing, he used a stiffer, narrower foot. To climb a rock wall with narrow crevices, he switched to a stiff foot with a rubber nub on the end that he could jam into the cracks. For ice climbing, he used a foot fitted with a neoprene bootee and crampons.

In competitive rock climbing, the various routes up a cliff are rated from 5.0 to 5.13 according to difficulty. Few climbers are able to do anything above 5.10. Hugh is doing 5.10 ascents, sometimes without ropes.

When asked by a reporter what it was like to climb now, as compared to the old days, he said, "Now my calves don't cramp."

He sees in the dark.

I have a psychologist friend who at the age of nineteen suffered a spinal-cord injury that left him wheelchair dependent. After that trauma, he completed college and graduate school and became a recognized expert in rehabilitation medicine. Once I asked him if, given the current improvements in surgical technology, he could again have the opportunity to walk, he would go for it. He said, after only a moment's hesitation, "I'd have to think about how much I'd be willing to give up."

He sees in the dark.

Stephen Hawking, the brilliant British cosmologist and astrophysicist, suffers from a degenerative neurologic disease, amyotrophic lateral sclerosis, that has left him immobilized and speechless. Yet he lectures worldwide using a computer-enhanced voice. In addition to his scientific writings that have shed light on how the universe was formed, he has also written a best-selling book on the subject for general audiences.

I saw him on a television talk show, a wizened, Yoda-like elf scrunched up in a wheelchair. Asked about the impact of his disability he said, "You know, what I do is, I think. I spend my life thinking and theorizing; it's what I like most. Look how fortunate I am—I have my mind and nothing to distract me from doing what I do best."

Now he just looks like Yoda to me.

He sees in the dark.

Don't identify too strongly with what you now know; that "truth" is impermanent. Identify with the possibility that at every moment you can emerge from your blind self to see in the dark.

8

SO WHAT'S NEW?

▲

When addressing my medical colleagues, I used to dread the question-and-answer periods because I expected the inquiries to be antagonistic, although only some were. Finally, I recognized that what people ask almost always says more about what they want to say than it does about what they want to know. Now I hear their queries a bit differently, more as statements that are disguised as questions, so I get less defensive.

After one such meeting a doctor asked whether anything I'd said was really new. I asked him if he'd heard anything new and he said no. "Is that okay?" I asked. He said yes but that he had hoped to learn something he didn't already know, something new. I said, as uncritically as I could, that if I didn't see something new every day, it was because I wasn't looking.

I learned this most clearly from people who are terminally alive. I was in San Francisco one day and found myself with some ex-

▲

SO WHAT'S NEW?

tra time. I called Jerry Jampolsky, a distinguished psychiatrist, and founder of the Center for Attitudinal Healing, who lives in Tiburon, California. The center is a place where individuals and families who are confronting life-threatening diseases and debilitating illnesses have a chance to be together and support each other. I told him that I'd read about his work and was interested in what he was doing. I asked if I could meet with him? Without a moment's hesitation, he invited me over the Golden Gate Bridge into the rolling green hills of Marin County that overlook San Francisco Bay.

Jerry and I talked briefly in his office. Then he said he didn't know anything that I couldn't learn better from the people in a group that was scheduled to meet in a few minutes. He asked if I'd participate.

I find myself in a group of twelve people, some sitting on old rocking chairs, others on threadbare couches, a couple cross-legged on the floor. The group is led not by doctors but by people who are confronting or have confronted catastrophic illnesses. The meeting begins by people introducing themselves in turn.

Next to me on the couch is a young man in his early twenties who's just been released from the hospital following a bout with pneumonia. He says he can handle whatever happens to him but he's having difficulty with his mother, who is always in panic and despair when she hears about his problems. It's so painful for him to watch her re-

111

sponse that he can't tell her about his repeated hospitalizations. Then he says he has AIDS.

Reflexively I move my leg away from his. Of course, he feels the movement, but he says nothing. After he has spoken, he leans over and whispers, "You can't catch it from my knee." I'm embarrassed that he can hear the language of my heart. Your unconscious mind speaks a language people can hear even when your conscious mind hasn't articulated the words. Now it's my turn to introduce myself.

Already the guy next to me knows I'm scared, and I feel guilty that I'm not really sick enough to be here. Then it becomes clear to me that the question really is, am I healthy enough to stay? So I tell the group, too sheepishly, that I'm a doctor who wants to learn more about confronting my fears and helplessness when dealing with people who are critically ill.

The next man says, "Hi, I'm Sam," and then buries his head in his hands and weeps. No one interrupts him, no one brings him tissues, no one jumps in. He finally says, "I'm thirty-five years old and three weeks ago I discovered a lump in my belly." While on a hike, he'd bent over to pick up his four-year-old son to put him on his shoulders and felt a sharp stabbing pain in his right side. When he felt the spot he noticed a lump. The following day, his doctor also felt the lump.

The doctor thought the lump was on the liver because it moved when Sam took deep breaths. He ordered X-rays and

▲

discovered a grapefruit-sized tumor in Sam's liver. The doctor stuck a needle in it and when the results came back from the pathologist, he told Sam he had liver cancer.

Generally, a liver tumor doesn't spread to other parts of the body as fast as it expands within the liver itself, ultimately disrupting the blood flow to the whole body. Sam tells the group that he feels healthy, that he can't believe that this is happening to him. He still lifts weights, he says, he's still hiking with his son, he feels strong and he's in the prime of his life. And then, his voice rising with anger, he says, "There are bums, derelicts, and dropouts out there. Why not them?" And then his tears give vent to his rage.

Sam says he got a call yesterday telling him the doctors are ready to do the liver transplant now. The biopsy report revealed that his disease was already invading his biliary system. He was told he should be available at a moment's notice. He had thought there was lots of time to decide.

He says to the group, "I don't see a light at the end of this tunnel, it's just an illusion. There is no light at the end of the tunnel!" he cries. I want to reach out to him but I feel I don't have the right. Nobody else gets up either.

After moments of painful silence a young man, perhaps in his mid-twenties, finally speaks up. In a tone neither consoling nor patronizing, he says that he has had a bone-marrow transplant. Sam looks up, still cradling his head. John says that over a year ago he had a fever, was weak and tired, and went to see a doctor who took some blood. The

▲

doctor discovered he had leukemia. After a bone-marrow biopsy they discovered it to be a particularly virulent form of the disease, and soon he was totally incapacitated by his treatment.

He did pretty well for a short time but then had a recurrent leukemic crisis. His doctors considered him too poor a risk for a marrow transplant, even though his brother was a compatible donor. The state of California, with limited funds for medical treatments, was facing a quandary that confronts every state, every insurer, and every hospital in this nation. This patient represented too great a surgical risk and the likelihood of his survival was so slim that the state decided its resources could be more fruitfully spent elsewhere.

Enraged, John decided to fight the state's decision. He called his congressman and had all of his friends send letters and telegrams. In the middle of this campaign his leukemic crisis dissipated. Once he was in remission the doctors decided to go ahead with the surgery and his brother donated the marrow. And here he is in the room telling Sam this story.

"It's been nine months since the surgery," John says. Looking at Sam he says, "When I was at my lowest, I said those exact words, 'I don't see a light at the end of the tunnel.' I saw no light until I decided that no one was going to deny me my last hope, which was surgery."

Walking over to Sam, John looks right in his face and says, "The light at the end of the tunnel is not an illusion. The tunnel is."

▲

• • •

It's hard to describe the intensity of this revelation; I am so awestruck by this insight. I'd never seen it that way before. It's not the events on your life's journey that make the difference between your being a victim or a hero. It's how you respond to them. The tunnel of fear is no more real than the light of hope.

So what's new is how we choose to see. It turns out that choice is the greatest power. Most of us minimize our choices by accepting somebody else's definition of what's possible or probable. The result is that other people's probabilities become our only possibilities.

We always have choices, even in situations that seem absolutely choiceless. Victor Frankl, the distinguished Viennese psychiatrist and Holocaust survivor, tells this story. He was brought to Auschwitz after being sealed for days in a railroad car. Upon arrival he was lined up for the infamous selection procedure: the weakest prisoners were sent to the gas chamber immediately, the stronger to forced labor. For the moment his life was spared and he was marched to a central gathering place. A starving man next to him stepped on an insect and then bent down to pick it up to eat. A Nazi guard spotted the man, approached him with his truncheon raised, and beat him to death on the spot.

At that moment, Frankl made the choice that ultimately saved his life. He knew he had little choice about whether he'd be selected to die, or about the means by which it could happen—whether he'd be tortured, beaten, starved to death, electrocuted, or gassed. What he did know was that, whatever they decided, he could choose to maintain his dignity. Even in his enslavement, that moment reminded him he still had choice—they could snuff out his life breath but they could not steal his spirit.

My friend Jerry Coffee was shot down over North Vietnam and spent seven years in a Hanoi prison. As long as he asked himself, "Why me?" he was filled with a sense of hopelessness. Not only couldn't that question be answered but it took him away from any awareness of the choices he had. It was only when he said, "Help me get through this day," that he knew that he could survive the moment. It is in our choices that we shape our destiny—not in lamenting our fate. Events in life are neither good nor bad, they are both.

So what's new? Only how we choose to see. As we learn more about susceptibility to disease and our ability to fight it, we discover that emotions probably run the show. It's our feelings that will most influence our destiny; it's what the heart believes, not what the mind thinks, that determines the course of our lives. Which is why it's possible to commit ourselves wholeHEARTedly to something, even when our mind is only half-sure it'll work.

Fear and hopelessness collude to steal our spirit until we can no longer see in the dark.

Children can help us remember how to dream.

In Phoenix, a seven-year-old boy with leukemia had a long period of remission after his initial treatment. After a year, he had a relapse. He was placed on high doses of toxic medications that left him extremely weak. When his breathing became irregular, the doctors thought he would soon die.

His mother called the Make-a-Wish Foundation, which grants

▲

last wishes to dying children. Her son had always wanted to be a fireman, so arrangements were made for him to leave the hospital for a day and visit a Phoenix fire station. The anticipation and fanfare alone were enough to rally him.

At the firehouse, the firefighters took him for a ride through the city streets on a hook and ladder truck with sirens blaring. His face was bright, even though his body was limp. After the ride, they had a special ceremony for him at the firehouse. They gave him a fireman's hat and a jacket with their battalion insignia on it and his name embroidered over the pocket. Every firefighter shook his hand and welcomed him as their newest member. It was the happiest day of his young life.

Back in the hospital, he improved enough to be discharged for several weeks. But when his breathing became gasping and irregular he was readmitted. Now he was only intermittently conscious. His mother, sensing that the end was near, asked the nurse if her son could see the firemen again. The nurse, who knew how important the visit to the firehouse had been to the boy, agreed to waive the two-visitors-at-a-time requirement.

When the mother called the fire station to ask them to come over, the firemen said, "We'll do better than that. Unlatch the window to his room and tell the nurse to announce over the loudspeaking system that patients should not be alarmed by the sirens. It's just the Fire Department coming to pay respects to one of their own."

Within minutes, everyone heard the approaching hook and ladder by its sirens. Roused by the sound, the boy awakened to see the firefighters climbing through his hospital window. In the arms of one of them, he asked weakly, "Does this really mean I'm a fireman?" To which the firefighter responded, "You always were." That night the boy died.

So what's new? Most of us don't become what we can be because we can't see it's what we already are.

9

KEEP ON SUCKIN'

▲

At the dinner table one evening, my daughter announced, "My teacher sucks." "Excuse me," I asked, thinking that suck is a verb and has to refer to something. "She sucks what?"

"She just sucks, Dad—it means she's terrible, she really stinks." Then in a trailing mumble my daughter added, "You are such a geek."

Sucking has become a bad word. Teachers suck, you suck, the world sucks. This is a crying shame because sucking is good. Sucking is how we come into the world and how we are sustained— first, sucking air, then sucking milk. How did this nurturing behavior get such a slanderous reputation?

I have the sense it's because sucking has come to mean that you are attached to something or someone other than yourself and therefore not functioning at optimal self-sufficiency. In contemporary life, if you are sucking it means you're suffering from a dis-

▲

ease called dependency. This is nonsense! All of us have dependent needs, and seeking to fulfill them isn't a disease. We are not always number one and doing our own thing; sometimes we're sick and afraid and would like someone else to paddle our canoe. Feeling dependent is part of being human; that's how we come into the world and, hopefully, it's how we go out. Dependency is different from the neurotic condition of codependency, in which you submerge all your needs to fulfill someone else's.

Everybody is dependent because nobody makes it alone. That's why we all have belly buttons—to remind us that we were once attached to and dependent on someone other than ourselves.

I believe the task in our lives is to find good things to suck from. Something that always makes us smile, that fulfills us, sustains us. Sucking was never intended to serve as a reminder of our insufficiencies and fears. It's when you suck to cover them up and when you have no strong sustaining connection to something other than yourself, that you get addicted. You can't find outside what you don't have inside. The widespread problem of addiction in contemporary American life exists because there are so few credible nurturing norms that we can suck on. We suck on booze, drugs, sex, and other addictive behaviors because we think they serve as a substitute for our unmet needs.

As a society, we've made a habit of sucking on a bottle of distilled spirits instead of the real thing. The real undistilled spirit, that ineffable force that propels us forward in the hard times, is waning. Because all the institutions that once sustained us, the pillars of our society—families, community, politicians, religious leaders, doctors, space engineers—have been found to be hollow, even corrupt. It's hard to believe in anything anymore. We've become self-absorbed, looking out only for ourselves. Divorce is as commonplace as marriage. More children are being raised without both biological parents in the home than with them. Lying is commonplace, from the White House to corporate boardrooms to the sacristy. We believe in nothing. Whatever a politician says we find suspect; even if one were to tell the truth, we wouldn't believe it. If a priest is a pedophile, it's no longer suprising; if facts are falsified, by space researchers, doctors, or financiers, we shrug.

In a society without an ethic of morality, those in power begin to make up their own codes of conduct. And among the rest of us, morale sags. Without sustaining connections with institutions or shared beliefs in something powerful, we become a society without a concept of good or evil. All actions are weighed in terms of expedience: Does it make sense for me right here and now? The result is that we become callous or worse—numb.

I read this story on the front page of *The Wall Street Journal*: Andrew and Laura Mae Cole were inseparable for almost fifty years. They'd lived in the same house in their small Florida town for that entire time, until they moved into a retirement home the year before.

Mr. Cole, ninety-three years old, still gave his wife a single red rose for no special occasion, picked out her clothes, and left her side only when she napped.

Then Mrs. Cole became bedridden. Under Florida law she couldn't stay at the retirement home any longer because it had no license to provide highly skilled medical care. She had to go to a nursing home alone because Mr. Cole wasn't frail enough to qualify and he couldn't afford it otherwise. The nursing home administrator fought for them, even wrote to the governor, who promised he'd do all he could to keep them together. Their doctor said he'd care for them where they were but that separating them would cause Mrs. Cole to slip away even more rapidly.

In the end, the authorities decided the rules were clear and that this sick lady's right to proper treatment was being denied. The authorities told Mr. Cole that, whether he went with her or not, they were going to take her to the nursing home, and they did.

He visited her every day, assuring her that she'd soon be out and they'd be back together again. Every time he left she called out to him, "I miss you."

Three weeks after she was moved, Mrs. Cole died. Mr. Cole was not there.

When we subordinate what's right to "the rules," we show disdain for humanity.

This man and woman were married for forty-six years. Their union represented the fulfillment of a cultural dream, enduring love, commitment in sickness and in health, till death do us part. Another myth was crushed.

In the absence of meaningful connections and sustaining beliefs we pursue instead material wealth, gambling, liquor, and drugs to ease our aches. Addictions are escalating in our culture. They are the topical anesthetic to an underlying pain. Addictions offer only momentary relief; they never sustain.

All addictions create a combination of feeling good and temporary relief from internal discomfort, but addicts eventually find that they can't control the behavior. Today, addictions are our most common and costly psychiatric problem.

In 1989 I spoke to a group that was also addressed by Donald Trump. "The Donald" told the audience that the reason the United States had deteriorated as an economic world force was because it had given away its power. More specifically, he said, the U.S. has given away its economic superiority to the Japanese and Germans by not demanding reciprocity for having lowered trade barriers to their goods, thus giving them an unfair advantage. Whatever credibility that argument may have, Trump's solution to the problem was to advise the group to study the leadership skills of Attila the Hun—essentially, if you want it, you have to take it. Take whatever you want, then put your name on it to remind you that you've got it.

What The Donald doesn't know is that when you do that you really don't have it at all . . . it has you. Holding on to things rather than beliefs is going to kill us.

The whole world has become an interdependent community. It's not us against them; instead, economic and planetary survival are predicated on recognizing our global connectedness. We cannot survive with the morality of plunderers.

The Trumps of the world are addicted to power and acquisition. Another addiction—gambling—is also growing, mostly because of the belief that good luck will bring limitless wealth. Gambling has become acceptable in state lotteries. And new casinos are springing up in Nevada, Maryland, New Jersey, and now on Indian reservations.

▲

My friend Flora is not a high roller. She has never placed a bet with a bookmaker and she has not borrowed untold millions from moneylenders. She is a sixty-eight-year-old Native American woman who plays bingo on her reservation seven days a week. She is losing money she cannot afford to lose. Unlike The Donald, she is not gambling with the bank's money. Her gambling began five years ago when her daughter was jailed on her third driving-while-intoxicated charge, this one resulting in a fatality. Flora had taken care of the grandkids plenty before, but now she had them full time. Another family to raise at her age was just too much for her. Bill, Flora's diabetic husband, pleaded with her not to play bingo every night, but since both of his legs have been amputated, he can neither chase her nor hold her back. Flora and Bill are in debt; she collects aluminum cans for cash and spends her periodic tribal allotment check on her bingo addiction.

Flora believes all of the ads and the hype that tell her "it only takes a dollar and a dream" or "you can't win if you don't play." Flora knows that the chances of winning are minuscule, but she nurtures "the big win" fantasy. It's a pretty typical history.

At first, the bingo was an escape from the house, a chance to get some breathing room from her invalid husband and her demanding grandchildren. Then she won a big jackpot and—*bang!*— she was hooked. Now she's chasing the losses that followed. She "knows" her luck will repeat, but it hasn't, and now she can't stop— she's addicted.

It's estimated that almost three hundred billion dollars was spent on gambling in the United States in 1990. That's about what our national debt is. Gambling is legal in forty-eight states. In the more than thirty states with lotteries, $20.8 billion was spent on tickets in 1990.

On America's Indian reservations, which have the lowest per capita income in the country, Native Americans are betting that gambling casinos on their lands, outside of federal tax regulations, will bring them much-needed outside capital for improving their lot. Reservations in the East have sued and won the right to hold high-stakes games. The Mohawks in New York and Canada are in a virtual civil war over this issue. Some recognize that supporting an addiction economy will ultimately destroy their culture, and others say they need it as a source of income. Either way, when an addiction sucks you in, it's always at the expense of your spirit.

Some people are addicted to food. We are becoming a nation afflicted with eating disorders. Bulimia, anorexia, and compulsive overeating are diseases that only a generation ago we hardly knew. Our worship of slim, beautiful, hard bodies and looking good has spawned an industry of diet and fitness products. It has also spawned addictions.

Bulimia is a compulsive eating disorder characterized by overeating binges usually followed by purging by vomiting and/or abuse of laxatives. Anorexia is a loss of body weight through self-starvation so exaggerated it can threaten life. Anorectics think they gain control over their lives by starving themselves.

Both anorexia and bulimia are perversions of a basic need to maintain life. People with eating disorders don't just eat to sustain their bodies. They use hunger and satiety as ways of feeling empty or full in spirit. Food becomes the prime ingredient for emotional barter: I'll feed myself when I feel lonely, empty, or worthless; or, I'll punish myself for my gluttony. Of course, bulimic behavior surfaces only in societies with a plentiful food supply; it is unknown in sub-Saharan Africa.

The disease particularly affects young women. What is the problem?

Some researchers theorize it's because women have become disconnected from their sustaining norms. Today they experience conflicting role expectations beginning early in adolescence and continuing through life. Be a cheerleader! Be successful, independent, beautiful, athletic, thin, elegant! Become a professional, get married. Be a mother, and do it all!

A society that devalues sustaining connections, that overemphasizes autonomy and self-discipline is a society able to define success by appearance.

Sally was a cheerleader in high school. She was appealing, socially sought after, and always dieting to make or keep her body "perfect." Her prominent father placed a premium on appearance. When she was eighteen, her parents separated, and she was devastated. She believed that her failure to achieve more, to have pleased them more, might in some way have contributed to their separation.

A year later, while her parents were finalizing their divorce, Sally's college boyfriend left her. Her self-confidence was shattered. She began to binge and purge. She went on to graduate school still looking good. She was an attractive, composed, competent young woman on the outside, but underneath Sally was crippled by doubt and by bulimia.

▲

When her loneliness became unbearable Sally came to see me. To avoid the pain of repeated abandonment, she made food her only companion. Her addiction became so overpowering that the only way she could "control" her compulsion was to vomit after eating. She finally kicked the habit when she rejected appearance as the most important commodity of exchange and learned how to develop real friendships. Food then lost its power over her.

I won't tell you about all the drug addicts and alcoholics I've seen. I'll only say that underlying all addictive behaviors is a common pathway that can be described in the language of biology or psychology. It tells us that we need pleasure. Eating, drinking, sex, and gambling are all pleasurable pursuits and healthy *in moderation*, but not to excess.

The answer is to stay in balance. Sometimes you work, sometimes you play; sometimes you give, sometimes you get; sometimes you hurt, sometimes you heal. Nobody does or feels any one thing all the time; it's not the way of the universe. Balance and harmony are the keys to health, not excess and pain.

Here's an example of a way to balance and health. Called the "time-dollar" revolution, it was the vision of a couple of nationally known liberal warriors.

Edgar Kahn, a University of Miami law professor, had the inspiration a few years ago while in a hospital bed recovering from coronary bypass surgery. His wife, Jean Camper Kahn, a lawyer who helped inspire the 1960s War on Poverty and civil rights struggle, died of cancer just after their book describing the program was published.

While recovering from surgery, Edgar reflected about all the people we put on the scrap heap—the elderly, minority teens, single heads of households. Feeling like scrap himself, he thought, "There are all these needs out there, there's got to be some way to put people and needs together."

So in 1987, the Kahns started a program in Miami and expanded it into a three-year experiment that included Boston, New York, and San Francisco. It's been miraculously successful and it's so simple.

The program has no bureaucracy. It's based entirely on volunteer efforts. A coordinator tells other volunteers about people who need something. If you have some time, you drive old George to see his doctor. It takes an hour; you've just earned a time dollar; it's tabulated in the coordinator's computer. You volunteer your time and provide services ranging from companionship, light housekeeping, rides to church and supermarkets, letter writing, reading to the blind, pet care, teaching, and you earn time dollars that you can redeem if you ever need help. The time you've given is the time you get.

Retired bank presidents who would never mow a lawn for money will work for time dollars. They also learn they can accept help more easily if they ever need it someday. Everyone in this cooperative program is equal because one person's time is valued the same as another's. It creates community, it extends families.

This is how we thrive, this is the antidote to addictions—building community, weaving relationships—getting connected. That's what sucking is about. Fill your spirit with it.

▲

10

THE TRANSFORMATION
OF GARBAGE

▲

I have a friend in Chicago, named Kay, who is an actress, singer, and playwright. She is also crippled by a long-standing anxiety disorder, which has resulted in an addiction to prescription drugs. Sometimes she doesn't emerge from her house for weeks. Immobilized by terror, she withdraws from all contact, lies in bed, or collapses on the floor in helpless despair. She has been through a parade of therapies for twenty years during which she has met with analysts, mystics, and psychopharmacologists. She is now studying t'ai chi with an expatriate Chinese monk.

An extraordinarily bright woman, she has more than a passing familiarity with psychological theories and their relationship to behavior, the immune system, and contemporary neuroendocrine research. Still, her scholarship and erudition have not yet afforded her an explanation for her experience.

I tell her she doesn't have to make sense of her reality, she just needs to learn how to adapt to it. That's what survival is all about.

▲

You don't have to understand it, just experience it and deal with it. You'll never be able to run away from it, so learn that the ordinary flow of all experience is movement toward resolution. Scientists call this homeostasis. The best way to deal with garbage is to handle it moment to moment.

If you're trying to grab the brass ring of eternal happiness, you're not going to get it. People who inherit millions are rarely joyful. Psychosocial researchers evaluating the fate of lottery winners discovered that the winners were ecstatic immediately after winning; after six months, less so; and after a year there was little or no difference between how they felt about life before winning and after. When it comes to sustaining joy, it turns out that the people who are most happy are the ones who are happiest most.

We must find joy in the small triumphs, in those good days, in the moment-to-moment changes. We must find more ways to experience joy in those day-to-day, repetitive, ordinary tasks and trials that make up life.

Kay was writing a play set in Indian country, so I invited her to come with me on a trip. She said she wasn't sure she'd be well enough, and then asked if she could cancel at the last minute if she panicked. I said no, she couldn't cancel. This was a time to be together, whatever the moment brought was the way it would be. I promised her that the experience would make sense.

I took her to see a friend in Hopi country, north of Phoenix.

On the way up we stopped in Oak Creek Canyon, a spectacularly magical place of red stone canyons, hidden waterfalls, and Indian ruins that once was the stopping place on the Hopis' migration to their current home. We stopped to gather cottonwood roots to bring to my friend, a kachina carver. Joe carves the roots into replicas of the kachinas, the spirit messengers who carry prayers from the Hopi people to the Creator. The kachina societies transmit to each generation the traditions that define the ritual and ceremonial life of the Hopi and allow them to carry on as a tribe. The Hopi also believe that the prayers keep the rest of us alive too.

As we gathered the exposed roots in the streambed we came upon a tree encircled at its base by an ancient automobile tire that, with age, had hardened like stone. Directly through this piece of debris had grown a twenty-foot tree. Kay and I both stared at it. Finally she said, "From that eyesore life grows." After a long silence, she said, "I think I've got it. Being healthy is just letting life grow through your garbage."

That's it. Most of us are into shoveling garbage rather than transforming it. We move our garbage from one pile to another as if we're really doing something about it.

Our task in life is not to lament, rationalize, and obsess. It is to get on with it. If you discard your garbage, then a tree can grow through it.

Kay and I went to Walpi, maybe the oldest continuously inhabited village on this continent. A towering rock altar stands in the village plaza, it is said to be the source of emergence of the first people who came here. A few of the people still live here all year round, and it's still quite "primitive," although most of the villagers have moved to newer quarters and only come back to these ancestral grounds for ceremonial occasions. Near this stone altar lives an ancient great-grandmother, over a hundred years old, some say. She asked us to come in. Her hands are arthritic but she is a working potter. She not only throws the pots but paints them afterward. I asked her how she manages to do it, since her knuckles are knotted by arthritis and she is nearly blind with cataracts. She said, "It's not my hands that make the pot, it's my spirit. My hands are broken but my potteries hold my soul, and that's whole."

From nothing grows something.

I bought the only piece she had left. It is a double-necked wedding vase, but cracked where the spouts are joined. "It's cracked," I said. "Me too," she said. "What about you? Aren't you a little cracked?" On their wedding day, lovers see only perfection in each other, but they will soon look again and see the cracks. If they can stay and see beyond the cracks, then they see the light.

Kay heard this as another transformation story: It's not our cracks that make us garbage. It's choosing not to see the light through them.

As we left this great-grandmother's house, Kay saw two small pieces of wood outside, sharpened on one end, wrapped together with yarn and small feathers. I told her to leave it alone, that it was a prayer offering. "I want it," Kay said. "It's discarded." Kay took it as a remembrance of this experience. This object, this discarded bit of garbage, will be a reminder about how she learned to transform garbage.

At the home of my friend Joe, the carver for whom we gathered the cottonwood roots, I tell him about the old tire, its new growth, and how it spoke to us. I babble on and when I finish Joe remarks, "All of us make it out of garbage, if we make it." We eat, laugh, and leave. On the way home I tell Kay about Joe's garbage.

▲

When he was seventeen, Joe was involved in an automobile accident. He and three friends had been drinking heavily. On their way home, their pickup truck overturned and he was crushed beneath it. Barely alive when the paramedics arrived, Joe was flown to Phoenix. He had suffered a severe spinal-cord injury that left him a quadriplegic. Two of his companions had been killed in the accident.

It took months for Joe to acquire the strength and dexterity to move himself in bed. Slowly, some function returned to his arms and fingers; eventually he could get out of bed and maneuver himself into a wheelchair. After two years of rehabilitation, he returned to the reservation, a young man whose dreams were crushed not by the accident but by a growing sadness and rage that made him give up hope.

Joe's older brother lived with him. Melton was a severe alcoholic whose binges regularly landed him in tribal jail. When he was sober, he was an expert kachina carver. But he was a mean drunk. He would torment his crippled brother, saying he couldn't stand to look at him with all the tubes and bags hanging from his wheelchair. "You'd have been better off dead than to make me have to look at you."

Whatever the explanation for his brother's cruelty, its impact on Joe was dramatic. He began to hate Melton, and with revenge as his driving motivation, he started to improve. In one bedroom was a locked gun case housing a whole assortment of high-caliber weapons used for hunting. Joe was determined to develop his arm and hand movements so he could turn the lock on the gun case, pick up the gun, load the shell into its firing chamber, aim at

Melton, and pull the trigger to kill the cruel, torturous bastard.

Joe squeezed rubber balls incessantly. He practiced "finger dancing" with rubber bands to strengthen his fingers. He performed push-ups on his wheelchair to build up his arms.

Two years later, he was finally strong enough. One night, after the family had gone to bed, Joe waited by the front door, cradling the loaded rifle and waiting for Melton to return from a binge. In the early morning hours, after dozing off, Joe was awakened by the sounds of staggering footsteps and drunken giggles. Armed and ready, he rested the gun against his abdomen, put his finger on the trigger, and when the door opened, he fired.

The bullet went directly through the heart of Melton's best friend, who had entered the house first. He was dead by the time he hit the ground. Melton walked in a fraction of a second later. He stared at Joe, open-mouthed with horror and fear.

Joe dropped the weapon and told his brother, "It was you I wanted dead." The FBI, which handles major crimes on Indian reservations, arrested Joe and charged him with first-degree murder. That's when I first met him.

The feds knew the whole story and did not consider it necessary to incarcerate this twenty-one-year-old quadriplegic. They were willing to place him in a rehabilitation facility if he would agree to see a psychiatrist. Initially, we met because they wanted an "expert" opinion as to whether Joe was insane when he committed the act. Later, we got together because we liked each other.

Ultimately, Joe was convicted of manslaughter but was sentenced to serve only the time he had already spent in the nursing home. That was to be followed by regular consultations with a psychiatrist for a supervised probationary period.

Reluctantly, Joe returned home, where the alcoholic Melton still lived. But now, Melton treated Joe differently. He no longer cursed at him. After his binges, he just didn't come home. Melton even asked Joe if he'd like to learn how to carve kachinas, to which Joe answered yes. His hand skills, once honed by hatred, were now refined by spirit. Melton taught him how to prepare the wood, fit the pieces together, how to use the different knives. He was fitted with forearm and finger braces that provided him the support to do finely detailed carvings.

The Hopi believe the kachinas will bring harmony to the whole earth.

Here is another ending to the Cain and Abel story, this one about brothers who hate each other but find resolution and renewal.

"All of us make it out of garbage, if we make it."

Sometimes, when I speak to young audiences, I take Joe's kachinas with me. I ask, "How many of you think you could carve something like this?" Then I ask, "How many think you could carve this with one hand?" Then I ask, "How many think you could carve such a thing if you were a quadriplegic?" And then I tell them Joe's story.

Garbage is just a test we must pass to move toward new discovery. Sooner or later, all pain and vulnerability, all garbage, must be regarded as an opportunity for new learning.

Kay wants to write this story as an opera.

By the time we reach the edge of Hopiland, the setting sun plays red-orange notes on the darkening sky. Ahead, wisps of smoke tell of an outside fire. I tell Kay I'm going to stop there. I make her take the fetish she picked up over to the

▲

fire pit. We will cleanse it in this traditional way. We cleanse it from wherever it has been to come to her in a good way without any clinging to its previous place. She promises to feed it and care for it.

Kay laughs hysterically as she says through tears, "This sacred object is being blessed with smoke from garbage." Kay and I are standing in the village dump.

11
GOOD BELLY

▲

In the lush Central American jungles of Belize I found someone who may be the last of the true Maya doctor-priests. The
Maya are scattered in economically destitute villages throughout Mexico, Guatemala, and Belize. They live on the edges of
their ancient cities, disconnected from their extraordinary past.
Even in Belize, an open democracy where the Maya make up seventeen percent of the population, the schools do not teach Mayan
history.

At ninety-three, Don Eligio Panti is a famed healer, honored by
villagers and government alike. He lives in the village of San An-
tonio, a Mayan community of two thousand people in the mountain foothills of the Cayo District. Half of its houses are
thatch-roofed, with both their interior and exterior walls made of
poles simply lashed together. The preferred sleeping arrangement
is in a hammock. Women, the caretakers of daily Mayan tradition,

▲

walk the dirt streets wearing white blouses with embroidered cuffs and collars, spectacularly colored tiered skirts, earrings, and beaded necklaces.

Don Eligio's thatched hut contains, in addition to his hammock, hand-carved chairs and tables, an assortment of burlap sacks filled with roots, bark, leaves, and vines. He dispenses these medicinals from another, freestanding, single-room "consultation shack." His wealth of knowledge includes not only his familiarity with herbs (which are now, interestingly, being studied by American ethnobotanists) but also his direct Mayan inheritance of the prayers and rituals used in his healing ministrations. His treatment is sought out by patients from all over Central America. He is not only an acknowledged expert in conventional diseases but is also in contact with the Mayan spirits who guide his skill in counteracting witchcraft. This, he says, is a big part of his work.

I knew nothing of Don Eligio before coming to Belize. I went there to go diving and to explore ancient Mayan ruins. During my wanderings in the excavations near the Guatemalan border I asked the park attendant about what was left of traditional Mayan culture, especially healing practices. He happened to be a full-blooded Mayan who, in addition to his park ranger duties, was a nationally renowned marimba player. He responded to my query: "What's left is only my sadness at not having listened well enough to remember the stories and be able to tell them to my children." He was no longer fluent in his native tongue, and his children didn't speak it at all. He knew of only one person who continued to use the old ways of healing. It was his uncle Don Eligio Panti, who just happened to live in a small village on the road back to our lodgings.

Don Eligio's waiting room is a wooden bench outside his one-room palm-frond-roofed consultation shack. I waited there for the patient ahead of me to exit. Next to me sat a blond, blue-eyed, freckle-faced young man who appeared to be in his thirties. Surrounding us in the yard were similar-looking children speaking a version of German I didn't quite recognize. The whole scene looked like a Nordic travel poster. Under an orange tree stood a Nordic-looking young woman wearing a long dress and a lace cap; she seemed to be talking to herself. Looking at me coyly, she picked up the hem of her dress to reveal her thigh and giggled.

My benchmate, seeing her, whispered to me that she had been this way for the last six years. Continuing the conversation, I said, "You don't look Belizean." He said, "No, we are Mennonites." His community came here from the United States and Canada almost a hundred years ago. First they went to Mexico, then to Belize, escaping what they believed to be encroachment into their isolated lifestyle. He was born in Belize and speaks German, Creole, Spanish, and English. Today, he and the entire entourage traveled on Belize's truly primitive roads for five hours to visit with Don Eligio.

I asked him about the young woman. He explained that when she was fifteen, she started to talk back to her parents. She wouldn't do anything she was told to do and even tried to hit people. Then she began to stand at a window, mute, stiff, and totally immobilized. Over the last several years she'd started this business of lift-

▲

ing her dress. She was passed from family to family but eventually proved too unmanageable for everyone.

"She's a little better now since she saw Don Eligio six months ago," he said. Before the Mennonites brought her to Don Eligio, she had been seen by medical doctors in Mexico and Guatemala, but Don Eligio, he said, was the only one who did any good. "What did he do?" I asked. "He gave us some kind of root to boil into a solution to bathe her in. The women do it every night, and then they give her a tea to drink. Then the male religious elders burn incense. They wave it over her and she breathes it deeply." The Mennonite elders had come back for more herbs and incense.

The girl now stood motionless under the orange tree. She postured herself into a kind of t'ai-chi position and held it stiffly. The children played near her, undistracted by her bizarre presence. I stared at her. I hadn't seen such a classic picture of catatonia since medical school.

I told my benchmate that I was a doctor, as a matter of fact a psychiatrist, a doctor of the mind. He said, "Isn't it interesting that we should be here at the same time?"

My time with Don Eligio was rapidly approaching; I could hear him dispensing the medication with instructions and goodbyes. I asked my benchmate if, to his knowledge, the young woman had ever been on any other medications. He said no. I told him I would talk to Don Eligio about her case and that perhaps I too could do something to help her. I asked him to wait for me.

I enter the hut with my driver, who will interpret. Don Eligio speaks Spanish, although his preferred language is the

Mopan Mayan dialect. I am sitting in a single room about five by eight feet. I'm on a bench against one wall facing Don Eligio, who is sitting on a wooden chair opposite me. His elbow rests on a corner table on which are an assortment of herbs, a wash basin, and a candle. On the wall facing me is a framed certificate from the Belizean government declaring him a national treasure.

I introduce myself in my stumbling high school Spanish and explain that I'm a doctor interested in native medicine. I ask my interpreter to add that I have worked with Native healers in North America, and I come with respect and appreciation. Don Eligio nods as he listens. He has a full head of white hair and his eyelids are hooded, giving the appearance that he's dozing or in trance. He has no shoes on; he wears a collarless, white short-sleeved shirt that's buttoned to the neck, and his trousers are long cotton pants tied at the waist with a rope.

Wishing to maximize the limited time I have, and knowing there are others waiting in the orange grove, I want to ask pressing questions. Before I start talking about the young woman outside, I ask him (through the interpreter), "What is the most important thing you've learned to be able to heal?"

Don Eligio laughs and after a few moments he says, "The most important thing I know to be able to heal is not to take a cold drink on an empty stomach on a hot day." I look with puzzlement and a shrug at my interpreter, thinking that I've missed something in the translation. He looks at me with similar disbelief and shrugs. I figure maybe the question wasn't asked right, so I ask him to ask Don Eligio again.

The old man nods and repeats it. Now I laugh too. I'm looking for the eternal seed of truth, some philosophical pearl, and the old man tells me the secret of the healing mystery is not to take a cold drink on an empty stomach on a hot day. And he's laughing. "What does this mean?" I ask. After a long time, Don Eligio responds, "Because it gives you Bad Belly."

"Bad Belly?" I ask incredulously. And he says, "Yes, Bad Belly. You can't heal if you have Bad Belly."

I knew that, but I just couldn't tell the story as well. Doctors often come to their patients with Good Head but Bad Belly because we are well trained in dispensing our technology but less efficient in sharing our humanity. We've reduced the healing equation to a single dimension, *knowing it* at the expense of *feeling it*. We come to people with Good Head but with Bad Belly, sometimes even no belly at all. As scientists, we have learned to subordinate the truth of what we feel to the certainty of what we know. Patients feel this disconnection as distancing and then often lose faith in the whole process. That's why people are increasingly seeking consultation from other practitioners, some of whom are great and some of whom aren't.

Contemporary medical training arms us factually but numbs us emotionally. This leads to people's distrust of doctors, which is reflected in the rise of malpractice suits. People are angry at the

▲

sad truth that you can be a doctor and not be a healer. A good doctor can make the right diagnosis and treat the patient, and if she's a great doctor, then she will also add a preventive component so the patient learns to minimize future exposure. But a healer can do all that and, in addition, help patients understand something about why they get sick, about their place in the world, and about their relationships with others, even the universe. We need to train at least as many bellies as we do heads.

In my own discipline, we psychiatrists pride ourselves on becoming more "phenomenologic," that is, being able to explain the phenomena of mental illness using objective markers like blood tests and brain scans that more reliably define disease. However, I find this model less useful in diagnosing and treating psychiatric disorders than other illnesses, because even if we could precisely define psychiatric illnesses, being able to treat them is a whole different thing. Giving an illness a name is not doing something about it. I once saw a young man of fifteen admitted to a local psychiatric hospital as an alternative to incarceration. Oren was first arrested when he was thirteen for involvement in a shoplifting incident. He was keeping watch outside while his friends went inside the convenience store. They packed their pants, stuffed their shirts, and left through a back door. However, they never came around front to tell Oren.

When his friends escaped out the back door, they triggered a silent alarm that alerted the police. Of course, the cops found only Oren; his friends were long gone.

As a result of that incident he received a probationary term during which time he again got into trouble. His friends dared him to throw a rock through the open window of a police car slowly moving by. He did it and hit the cop right in the head. Everybody ran, but the officer, having seen Oren cock his arm to throw the rock, caught only him.

His second probationary violation happened when he was caught by a security patrol on the roof of a new home construction site. This time he was hospitalized instead of being sent to a detention center. That's when I saw him.

Oren wasn't a bad kid. He wasn't dumb, either. He tested out normal; he wasn't cruel, hostile, or antisocial. Before seeing me, he'd been evaluated by a variety of learning specialists including child psychiatrists, psychologists, and testing experts. They diagnosed him as hyperactive, depressed, and suffering from a serious "personality disorder." They prescribed a variety of drugs, none of which had any real impact on him.

I saw no evidence of any of these diagnoses. Oren was naive, easily influenced, and made poor choices, but there was no evidence of major mental illness.

At the family meeting a week after his admission, his father wanted to know what Oren had. I told them he didn't belong in a psychiatric hospital; I also told them I didn't even think he needed medication. His father persisted: "What does he have? What is his problem? What do you call it?" Diagnoses, I said, are important only if they provide a specific treatment strategy. But the father demanded an answer: "What does he have?"

Exasperated, I finally said, "He's just a schmuck." There was a stunned silence, then his father broke into a grin and asked, stunned, "He's just a schmuck?"

"He's just a schmuck." I laughed. "That's it."

His father said, "I always knew that, but I thought maybe I was missing something because everybody was making it into a disease. A schmuck. A schmuck I can deal with." And he did.

After Oren's discharge, he went to an adventure-based summer program for kids in trouble, where he learned how to determine which friends he could trust with his life. He also learned how to depend on himself. Then he changed schools and did pretty well. Oren learned that being a schmuck is not a disease and that most of us grow out of it.

The great danger in giving things names in psychiatric practice is that we get the exaggerated conviction that when we have named something we also know how to deal with it. Diagnostic certainty is too often a way of convincing patients of *our* power and minimizing *theirs*. Our intention is not to overwhelm people into thinking we can do it to them; rather, we are here to join our patients in a collaborative effort.

Too often, we use our skills to defend ourselves from becoming overwhelmed by our patients' feelings.

William Styron, the distinguished American novelist, wrote a compelling little book entitled *Darkness Visible: A Memoir of Madness*, in which this very private man was driven to describe his own experience of depression.

He had all the typical markers—suicidal ideation, hopelessness, sleeplessness, overuse of medication and alcohol, even a family history of depression. But the *symptoms* by which we identify depression never adequately convey the central *experience* of it. Our phenomenologic pursuits have not helped doctors feel the experience of it. You cannot relate to people in healing ways if you only come to them with your head. You've got to bring your belly.

Styron was admitted to a psychiatric hospital where he received the standard assessment and treatment. He noted no improvement on medication, he thought group psychotherapy a farce, and he called art therapy "organized infantilism." The biggest problem was that Styron's doctor never talked to him about what he felt. Instead, the doctor talked about biological explanations, enzyme levels, hormonal responses, and genetics. In doing so, the doctor distanced himself further and further from Styron's experience. He was using inadequate scientific explanations to keep himself from having to face his patient's anguish. In the depths of his patient's despair, the "healer" expected Styron to accommodate to the medical definition of his patient's suffering.

Styron writes that in the "ferocious inwardness" of his pain, his doctor proposed to start him on yet another medication. The doctor explained the importance of diet and mentioned potential side effects, including impotence. This is Styron's description:

> Until that moment, although I'd had some trouble with his personality, I had not thought him totally lacking in perspicacity; now I was not at all sure. Putting myself in Dr. X's shoes, I wondered if he seriously thought that this juiceless and ravaged semi-invalid with the shuffle and the ancient wheeze woke up each morning from his Halcion sleep eager for carnal fun.

• • •

▲

This doctor had no idea what his patient felt. He had no concept of the depth of Styron's pain, the desperation of his emptiness. If he did, he never communicated it in a way that his patient could hear. And so the patient could neither trust the doctor nor believe that he could heal him. This is Bad Belly treatment.

Here's another example.

In the summer of 1989, at age sixty-nine, Anatole Broyard, an enormously talented literary journalist who, for fifteen years, was the daily book reviewer at *The New York Times* and later editor of the *Times Book Review*, was diagnosed with prostatic cancer. By the time it was diagnosed the cancer had spread to other parts of his body.

One year later, on August 26, 1990, Broyard wrote an article that appeared in *The New York Times Magazine* section entitled "Doctor, Talk to Me."

> *What do I want in a doctor? I would say that I want one who is a close reader of illness and a good critic of medicine . . . I would like a doctor who is not only a talented physician but a bit of a metaphysician too, someone who can treat body and soul. I used to get restless when people talked about soul, but now I know better. Soul is the part of you that you summon up in emergencies. You don't need to be religious to believe in the soul or to have one.*
>
> *I'd like my doctor to scan me, to grope for my spirit as well as my prostate. What would please me most would be a doctor who enjoyed me . . . a storyteller with a voice of*

his own, something that conveyed the timbre, the rhythm, the diction and the music of his humanity.

Not every patient can be saved but his illness may be eased by the way the doctor responds to him and in responding to him, the doctor may save himself . . . it may be necessary to give up some of his authority in exchange for his humanity, but . . . this is not a bad bargain. He has little to lose and much to gain by letting the sick man into his heart. If he does, they can share, as few others can, the wonder, terror and exaltation of being on the edge of being between the natural and the supernatural.

Seven weeks after the article appeared, Anatole Broyard died.

Sometimes I come from a Great Head/Bad Belly place too. Before completing this book, I sent a proposal outlining its contents to potential publishers. I wanted to write a piece that would demand serious attention from my colleagues, yet I feared they would reject the nontraditional lessons I had learned about healing. So I got stuck. When I find myself at such impasses, I often go to a sweat-lodge ceremony; it always helps me see through my belly. This time, during the opening round, I found myself becoming increasingly nauseated. My initial reaction was a desire to run out, but the expectation is that whatever you feel in sacred ceremonies is exactly what you are supposed to experience. Don't run away from it, the Indians say. Learn by looking straight at it right there in the presence of people and the Spirit.

I threw up, and the ceremony continued without a skip. Suddenly, looking into the pile of glowing lava rocks, I saw the round heads and faces of my medical professors hissing a steam of disapproval and it became clear to me that I had been writing only from my head. I was writing an objective, dispassionate clinical summary, pure Bad Belly. My prideful Yale-trained self was still afraid of not being taken seriously. So in the lodge I decided that I would say this as I truly feel it. A psychiatrist is a doctor of the spirit, someone who serves as a guide to the dispirited, one who becomes a vehicle for the restoration of faith.

Hour by hour, day by day, we allow life to steal our spirit. Too few of us—doctors and laypersons alike—believe in anything. Scientific insight and clarity will not help us reclaim a healthful balance in life; it is not the certainty in our heads that will save us but the truth of our hearts. What we ultimately know about life's journey is nothing—what we believe is everything.

What about the catatonic young woman in Belize? Don Eligio said that when she was fifteen, a young man tried to exploit her sexually. When he couldn't get his way, he used witchcraft on her; that's why the woman suffers. Don Eligio described the bathing solution as a way to cleanse her of the poison that the young man used to make her stiff. The herbal tea would clean her out internally. The family incense, a resin he gathered from the copal tree, was to be waved over her with a macaw feather so that she could breathe in the Creator's breath symbolically, which would purify her soul.

What a concept! Here it is in psychiatric language:

When ambivalences are crippling, the resulting pain can be-

come unbearable. We can escape their reality by creating another
that provides both explanation and relief. This young woman, in
the flower of her awakening, was confronted with her sexuality and
dealt with its tension by retreating into catatonia. The old name
for this disease was dementia praecox, a disease of adolescents
who go crazy as a defense against their emerging sexual selves.
Psychotherapy and drugs are the best ways psychiatrists have yet
found to deal with this problem.

Don Eligio knew this girl housed some kind of demon deep
within. He knew she'd been "poisoned" by a vindictive suitor. Don
Eligio had the power to rid her of the spell by washing away even
imaginary sins. Her bewitched behavior continually distanced her
from her extended family, so Don Eligio found a way that allowed
the community to welcome her as a child hoping to be reborn.

That's what we do in psychotherapy. We talk to patients about
these early traumas unjudgmentally and help them find the way
to heal so they can move into adulthood.

Don Eligio didn't talk to the young woman at all; he found a way
to get those who knew and lived with her to talk to her. Not just
with words either; he encouraged the women to touch her in a loving, nurturing way by bathing her as infant and then suckling her
with sweet tea. The community's religious elders, all men of good
intention, came to her with feathers and smoke and touched her
in a pure way. They brushed away the stain that immobilized her.
For six years, the community had only dealt with her through de-
mands or rejection. Since the treatment began, she had become
more receptive and obedient.

After I returned home, I sent some medicine to the community, emphasizing that it only be used in conjunction with Don Eligio's prescriptions. Three months after my return from Belize I received a letter from the brother of my benchmate in Don Eligio's yard. The letter was written in dialect German, the everyday language of the community, and said, "My brother asked me to write because he is afraid he doesn't write well enough. I don't either, but I'm doing my best. The girl you saw at Don Eligio's, her name is Sara. Your medicine arrived and it helps. Sara is smiling now, talks, moves without being pushed. Please send us some more medicine, I will be happy to pay for it. Goodbye for now. I would like to address you as True Friend and say thank you."

That's the most important thing to learn if you want to be able to heal. Good Belly is about making connections, between your head and your gut, and between you and your patient.

Unfortunately, the modern notion of healing goes back to the idea of asepsis. We doctors are taught we must avoid contagion; that if we get too close, we'll catch something. Too often we interpret that to mean that we must protect ourselves and those we come in contact with by creating sterile environments. The problem is, we've carried sterility a bit too far. We have sterilized our thinking to the point where we believe that we can't bring our "soiled humanity" to our healing. We are all soiled and we're all blessed. If you can't be real, you can't heal. This is the big challenge for us as doctors—to get connected.

It's important for all of us to remember that if we can't do it ourselves, it's not a sin; we just need to bring in somebody else who can. If you can't deal with healing the spirit, lots of good people out there can; invite them to join you.

Remember the time-dollar program. This is Edgar Kahn's poem to his wife, Jean, which serves as a dedication to their book, published shortly after her death. It could be a calling card for us all.

> All we have
>   in the
>   here and now
>   is our love for each other
>   our willingness to forgive one another
> and our willingness to come to each other's rescue.

12

LEARNING HOW
TO PRAY

▲

I called Bill Tyner "Sigee," Uncle. We first met in a Native American church meeting, where we sat side by side in a tipi all night long. In the early morning hours he had asked me to drum for him, an invitation to accompany his voice and rattle with my drumbeat.

I hesitated. I didn't want to look bad. What if I missed a beat? I'd be exposed to the group and I wanted to be great! Finally, I shook my head no and someone else drummed. After we emerged from the meeting, my Sigee came over and said, "When someone asks you to drum for them, you do it, even if you don't think you're ready. Don't let your head get in the way. If your head gets in the way you'll never learn how to pray. It's not by knowing it but by doing it that you learn."

In the short decade we knew each other, that's what he taught me, again and again. If you want to know it, don't weigh it—feel it.

▲

Prayer is how you stop thinking about yourself; prayer is the taming of the you.

It's a voice from the heart that goes directly to the tongue, it's a heart song. That's the difference between prayer and speech. Speech is a mind song. You think about it before you say it; you weigh it, you measure its impact and outcome before you let it out. When the lips and tongue are moved only by the mind, they lie.

It's always been hard for me to pray because I had a hostile-dependent relationship with God. The times I was most likely to pray were those during which I felt most terrified and vulnerable, and I hate feeling afraid. Praying at my weakest made me angry at God.

The tipi, not the synagogue, is where I learned how to pray. It was there I learned that God did not take pleasure in my fearfulness, nor did the Great Spirit, in order to feel powerful, require me to grovel. In the tipi I saw another connection to the Spirit, not an all-powerful, vengeful, vindictive Source but a loving presence everywhere; in trees, animals, clouds, even stones. It was there that I learned all things are filled with power and a spiritual energy. This awareness is the starting point for Native Americans in their understanding of the natural world.

Bill Tyner, a Shawnee spiritual elder, and Native people everywhere have never scientifically measured the energy of nature but claim they can feel it. For a long time, my training equipped me to measure things but prevented me from feeling them.

The first time I felt a stone, I mean really felt it, it sang to me with a perceptible pulsing energy. You may think this sounds rather strange, but it really happened on a recent visit to Jerusalem.

LEARNING HOW TO PRAY

My cousin arranged for us to see the guarded archaeological excavations underneath the Wailing Wall. The wall is the last vestige of the second temple in Jerusalem destroyed by the Romans in 70 A.D. about the time of Jesus' crucifixion. It is the most sacred shrine in Israel. It once surrounded the temple's inner courtyard, in which stood the Holy Ark. The Holy Ark reputedly held the stone fragments of the original ten commandments that Moses brought down from Mount Sinai. The Ark is also said to have contained the manna that fed the Jews during their exile from Egypt.

Historians say the Ark stood at the exact spot where the Mosque of the Dome of the Rock now stands. This mosque is the third-holiest shrine in Islam. It is from this Rock that Mohammed is said to have ascended to heaven on the back of a winged horse. The old temple walls surround the mosque. Observant Jews never go inside.

As a nation, Israelis have a passion for archaeological excavation; they view it as a living connection with their history. They would love to dig under the Rock, find the Ark, and look inside, but they can't get that close.

But their diggings have uncovered the foundation of the original Temple of Solomon. You can see the actual cornerstone embedded right in Mount Moriah. The descent through the dimly lit passages is a journey through two thousand years. We come upon an enlarged chamber. A member of the faithful is always there. Their prayers carry eerily through the subterranean tunnels. That day a pious Jew sang the ancient Hebrew prayers with a spine-tingling Arabic melody. This spot is the closest that a religious Jew may get to the Ark.

▲

Some of the stones that make up the base of the temple walls weigh more than twenty tons. It is mind-boggling to imagine how the builders fitted them together with such precision, without mortar or cranes. In a chamber beside the actual cornerstone is a smooth, six-foot-long yellow rock whose convex surface bulges out from the wall. When it was first discovered, archaeologists thought that perhaps the stone had fallen, but it fits in its place so perfectly that they decided such an accident was improbable.

My cousin asked me to touch the stone. I was surprised to feel it humming, like a low-level electrical current. I touched it with both hands—both of them buzzed. Then I touched it with one finger, then with my lips—they hummed. I asked my cousin, "Is it the singing of the faithful that's reverberating through the stone? Is it some kind of harmonic vibration? Maybe a subtle seismic event, a short in the electrical system?" Then, for the first time, I really understood what my Sigee meant when he said, "Don't weigh it, feel it."

I asked my wife to feel the stone; she didn't feel the humming. I touched it again, this time with my cheek, my forehead, my tongue; I still felt it. Around me the stones had smoke stains, living testimony of the burning of the temple two thousand years before. I could smell it.

I asked my cousin to tell me about the stone. He answered that scholars found no mention of the stone in the Torah. Then an archaeologist consulted an old Moroccan rabbi, who took one look and said, "It's an olive press. I remember one just like it in my village as a boy."

And it suddenly dawned on me that I was looking at the stone

▲

on the last day of Chanukah, the holiday that remembers the victory and rededication of the temple. The humming stone is an olive press. Virgin olive oil was collected from hand-pressing olives against it; only their first drop of oil was pure enough to fuel the lamp that burned continuously in front of the Holy Ark. These droplets were collected in a tiny gutter that emptied into a small cistern. Once the archaeologists knew what they were looking at, they found the collecting vault.

It was from this small reservoir that the victors obtained the oil to light the lamp that rededicated the temple after the defeat of the Syrians. I was sitting on the very spot at the same time of year, two thousand years later. This event of miraculous discovery and rededication is celebrated yearly as the Festival of Chanukah.

The power of the place sent a chill through me. I didn't understand why until the following day, when I wandered through the Museum of the Jewish Diaspora in Tel Aviv. On the second floor of the museum is a computer bank into which you can enter your family name or your family's hometown, and the computer prints out an entire history of the town or the name.

I punched in "Hammerschlag" and out came this: "This German-Jewish name, which means blow of the hammer, is a translation of the Hebrew word *makav* which means the hammer. [I didn't know that.] It is also the surname of Judah, the third son of Mattathias the Hasmonean (1 Macc.) who was the leader of the revolt against the Syrians."

Judah the Hammer! The previous day, I'd sat at the very spot where thousands of years before my ancestral namesake found a small reservoir of oil and where I first felt the aliveness of a stone.

▲

If you want to know it, don't weigh it—feel it.

Why is it so difficult to give up old perceptions when it's clear that what we really know is only a fraction of what there is to be known? The tiny fraction we see is not the only way it is.

Whenever we say "I know it," it means that we no longer want to struggle with other ways of seeing it. But the way we once saw it may not be the way it is now. Certainly the way something is now does not determine that it will always be that way because we are, all of us, on a journey whose ultimate destination is unknown.

As a species we want to know it, and we want to know it once and for all. But nobody's *got it*—we're all *getting it* because we're always coming to it from a new perspective. Every time we get the chance to reexamine our old certainties, we ought to do so with joy and gratitude, because what we truly know is only what we experience in the moment.

Plato told this story about the limited way in which we see things:

Slaves are imprisoned in a cave, chained together in such a way that they always face a wall. On the wall they see only shadows reflected from the cave opening behind them. Shadows of people, of animals, of an occasional charioteer rumbling by.

They spend their entire lives facing a wall, seeing shadows as their reality.

If the slaves were released from their captivity and taken to the cave opening they could look at the real-life figures on the roadway outside the cave, and through this new knowledge realize that their vision had been limited to what they could interpret from the shadows on the wall.

Those of us who choose to stay in our caves even after we are released are slaves. We want to see it only the way we know it. Being chained to our preconceptions leaves us no room for reconsideration.

Prayer is the best way I know to separate us from our preconceptions, because it comes from a feeling place within us, not a knowing place. Pay attention to your heart song; it's always closer to the real truth than the one in your head.

People sense it when you tell the truth, and they respond to you differently. They want to listen to your prayers, not your certainties, because they recognize your prayers as more believable.

A seventy-year-old Navajo woman who spoke no English found me in Phoenix—just by accident, said her daughter-in-law. Her daughter-in-law, Lorraine, and I had worked together at the Phoenix Indian Hospital for many years. One Sunday, she and her mother-in-law were on their way to a local hospital where the older woman was to undergo a hysterectomy for a cancerous uterus. The city's freeway system, undergoing major expansion, required detours and reroutings. Lorraine got lost. Her mother took all these changes as a signal that the surgery would not go well.

When Lorraine stopped at a convenience market to call for directions, I pulled up. I come to this place once a week to pick up a newspaper. Lorraine saw me and told me she was here with her mother-in-law and that the old woman was frightened and had a premonition about the surgery. Lorraine then introduced me to her mother-in-law, saying in Navajo, "This is a doctor I work with. He is also a singer."

I had never been introduced that way before and I liked it. Her mother-in-law smiled and brightened. She asked me through her daughter if I would sing for her and bless her before she went to the hospital. Then she would not be so afraid of the doctors and the hospital. She believed this was why we came together at this moment.

We all go back to my office and with an elk hide and seven round stones, I tighten the skin around a three-legged cast-iron pot. This is called "tying the drum." From my medicine box, I take an eagle feather and light some cedar. I touch the woman with the smoke, then Lorraine, then me, and the drum, and fan the smoke throughout the room.

There I am, sitting on the floor of my office singing and drumming, wondering what someone walking by my French doors would think. (Talk about having trouble being in the moment.)

I tell her in English (Lorraine translates): "I'm going to pray for you the best way that I know how [which was how my Sigee Bill Tyner always began]. I offer these prayers on your behalf so that only good things will happen to you, that the surgery will go well for you, so that the surgeon's hands will be guided by the healing power of the Creator. I offer these prayers so that the hospital and staff will treat you well, with respect, and that your journey will be easy."

And then I sing some songs. At the end, this beautiful old woman in her long dress, velveteen blouse, and turquoise necklace says to me, "I want to call you son." She takes a piece of jewelry with a deep blue turquoise stone from her purse and gives it to me.

*And that stone, too, hums in my hand. It is a healing
stone, she says. It comes from the place of my ancestors.*

Discovery doesn't only happen when you acknowledge that you're
lost. It also happens when you open yourself up to seeing.

Bob, a forty-nine-year-old attorney with lung cancer that had
spread through his body, called me. He was in his oncologist's office for a weekly chemotherapy treatment when he opened to an
article about my continuing medical education with Native American healers. He called and made an appointment to see me.

Six months earlier, when he was first diagnosed, Bob had asked
his doctor about his chances for survival. The oncologist said Bob
would probably be dead within a year. Bob didn't know whether to
hit the doctor or cry. He did neither. Now, six months later, he was
counting down, growing hopeless, and looking worse.

He needed somebody to talk to, and felt that finding the article
was no coincidence. He wanted to renew his faith.

"I'm just an ordinary man," I told him. "Not a sage, spiritual
leader, holy man, or miracle worker, but I'll work with you through
this time."

For the next three months we talked. Talked about what we knew
and what we feared. Talked about whether form is more important
than substance, and whether the body was just a temporary repository for the spirit within.

I told him about my experience with the stone in Jerusalem and
then about Lorraine's mother-in-law who had given me a stone that
she said held the healing spirit of her forebears. It came to her
from her mother, who got it from her mother, and so on, for who

knows how many generations. She felt as if that stone in its exact form held the substance of ancestral healing power. Bob asked to see it, so I took it out of its pouch and handed it to him. After some moments he looked at me and said, "I feel a hum." "Me too," I confessed.

> I want to give him the stone, so I ask him to keep it. "Oh no," he says, "I couldn't take it. It was given to you."
>
> "It's okay," I tell him. "You're supposed to have it—that's how it works. You get it, then you give it, which is the only way to know you ever had it."
>
> I light some cedar in an abalone shell and, as its fragrance fills the room, I tell him to remember the smell as I bless this stone that's now his. This leaf, which changes itself into aromatic smoke, will help him remember; to remember the stone, the hum, the essence of our gift, our spirit.

I was out of town during Bob's final week of life. I had told him I'd be away for several days, but would be back by the end of the week. I asked him if he'd be here when I got back and he nodded yes. "Why are you hanging on with this kind of pain?" I asked him.

He said, "I still have something else to learn."

Upon my return, I found a message on my answering machine from Bob's wife. Bob had been unconscious for twenty-four hours and she felt fairly certain he had little time left.

I went to his house and lit some cedar in the abalone shell. I said to him, in his comatose state, "Remember this smell. It will carry you, my friend, like smoke on eagles' wings to touch us all again."

I held his hand, and even though he was unconscious, I swear he squeezed my hand. An hour later, he died.

His widow sent me a tape some weeks afterward. She said Bob had made it for me with instructions to mail it after his death. It was his favorite tape, the Paul Winter Consort accompanied by the soundings of whales. Bob made an introduction to the tape: "Carl, I want you to sit down and light that cedar, lean back in your chair, and watch me on the cave wall. I am the Walrus. I am the Eggman. I am the Whale."

The songs of our hearts—prayers—are what give lift to hope.

The Hopi say that clouds are formed from the last breath of living things. Each cloud with its own shape is a reminder that the form comes and goes but its essence is transferable. Wood burns and becomes ash. And in being consumed by the flame, the wood gives off heat, which becomes moisture, which accumulates in clouds and showers rain, allowing the wood to reemerge as flowers.

I see Bob whenever a whale-shaped cloud goes by.

Prayer gives lift to the wings of dreams.

EPILOGUE

RECAPTURING THE SPIRIT

▲

There will come a time near the end of this world's life cycle when we will see a change in the pattern of life. The Hopi say it will be signaled by natural disasters and conspicuous consumption, that the obsession with seeking material goods will precede self-destruction.

The Hopi know this will all come to pass because today's patterns were planned by the Creator, Masauu, when the Hopi first emerged on this planet. The Hopi came here through a hollow tube from an underground dwelling place in the bottom of the Grand Canyon. At the time of emergence they were given a set of stone tablets onto which were inscribed the laws by which they were to live. The tablets also contained a warning; in time, they were told, they would be influenced to forsake the life plan that Masauu gave to them. If they abandoned their way, neither they nor the earth would be preserved.

"It's up to you," said Masauu. "All I have is my planting stick and my corn. If you are willing to live as I do and follow my instructions, then you will live here with me and take care of the land. And if not, blood will flow; the wind will speak with mighty breath; earthquakes, floods, famine will occur; and wildlife will disappear." All this has been foreseen.

So far, all of the Hopi prophecies have come true. They predicted the coming of "white brothers from the East"; they predicted the development of nuclear weapons, which they call "the gourd of ashes"; they even predicted the creation of the United Nations, which they call "the house of Mica."

Their last prophetic vision is that of purification. Now is the time. The Hopi say humanity must collaborate if we are to restore our existence on the planet.

Martin Gashwaseoma is the keeper of the ancient Fire Clan tablets in the Hopi village of Hotevilla. Like most traditionalists, he says he's not a leader, just a simple farmer. His uncle, Yukeoma, kept the Fire Clan tablets before him. As traditional leader of the village, Yukeoma resisted the government's pressure to abandon the old ways based on religion and clans and create a more democratic representative form of government and he was jailed because of it. Yukeoma met with President Taft in 1911 and appealed to him on behalf of the Hopi that the Creator's way was not being honored and soon war would come and then it would come again and again. Yukeoma was in and out of jail for nearly thirty years for obstructing the path to modernity.

In the winter of 1990, while the United States and its allies were preparing for a ground war in Iraq, Martin Gashwaseoma met with the governor of New Mexico to tell him that the time for purification had come. Martin told the governor that its beginning would occur in Santa Fe.

Santa Fe, New Mexico's capital, was once an old-fashioned frontier town but now has a population of 125,000. The Pueblo Revolt in 1680 began in Santa Fe when the tribes of the Rio Grande Valley rose up to rid themselves of the yoke of the conquistadors and the Catholic Church. They were quickly suppressed. This revolt was a critical juncture in the settling of the Southwest, and not a joyful moment for Native people.

Santa Fe sells more Indian artifacts and handmade crafts than anyplace else in the United States. At the beginning of this century art dealers were selling pots, blankets, jewelry, and other crafts made by Native Americans from the backs of trucks or carts. Later, fancy galleries were established and prices skyrocketed. In the last decade market sales have escalated dramatically. A Navajo "chief's blanket" that sold in the early 1970s for $1,200 was recently auctioned at Sotheby's in New York for over $500,000. Ironically, this fashionable appreciation of our Native American cultural heritage is also destroying it.

The owner of an exclusive Indian art gallery in Santa Fe was recently approached by a dealer offering an old Hopi ceremonial mask. This dealer, a white "Indian trader," is known by the Hopi elders to be disreputable. He comes to the Hopi villages waving money, asking for anything old (kachinas, pottery, weavings, artifacts). More than once he has been declared unwelcome, but he returns nonetheless. He also advertises in local newspapers and invites collect telephone calls from anyone who has something to sell. For the price of a few cases of beer, someone can steal any-

EPILOGUE

thing from the kivas (ceremonial chambers) and this white trader offers a readily accessible market.

Those who sell the Hopi culture to the trader are often Hopis, and this continued success mirrors the lost traditional values of the Hopi tribe. As prophesied, this seduction is crippling them, and their culture is slowly disappearing. The white man's "god"—gold—continues to lure them into separating the meaning from the object.

The Hopi themselves are becoming increasingly cynical about the value of their own ceremonies and symbols. For example, the tribal council in 1989 voted to build a road and gravel pit smack in the middle of the Snake Clan's gathering grounds. The tribal council, made up largely of modernists, was imposed on the Hopi by the federal government in 1936. Like Yukeoma, current Hopi traditionalists want to abolish the tribal council and replace it with a religious-based authority. As a result, rampant internal strife threatens the tribe's survival.

It is little wonder, therefore, that the Hopi police, the Bureau of Indian Affairs, law offices, and the FBI are investigating the disappearance of dozens and dozens of religious articles including masks, shields, kachinas, and effigies.

A member of Martin's village sold a 150-year-old mask to the "Indian trader" just a few years ago and he, in turn, sold it to a Santa Fe art dealer. The mask was particularly sacred, representing Wupamo, the guardian of the Bean Dance. The Wupamo mask is a round yucca fiber basket, three feet in diameter, covered with deerskin and crowned with braided corn husks. It's painted in red, black, green, and white earth pigments that give it a facelike appearance. Sticks bearing feathers protrude from its crown. The Hopi don't call this a mask; they call it Spirit Friend.

The Bean Dance signals the opening of an elaborate ceremonial season that forms the heart of Hopi religious life. Performed at the beginning of the kachina season, it ensures not only good crops but also the well-being of the village.

The dealer who bought the mask described it as "the greatest" he'd ever seen. He later told investigators that he asked the trader for a receipt to show that he had clear title to it but the receipt never arrived. The dealer kept the mask anyway. He had paid the trader $34,000, and in turn sold it to collectors for $75,000. The Hopi who stole it probably got no more than a couple of hundred, if that.

Soon after the dealer acquired the Wupamo he experienced an armed robbery, several major shoplifting incidents, and a murder/suicide in his store. The Hopi know this is what happens when you steal someone's spirit and sell it. They believe the mask is alive; in their village they would feed it because its spirit is in there. No individual can hold title to its living essence, so if you tamper with it you tamper with the life force and it will drain yours. They know it.

Before the new owners received their purchase, it was prominently displayed at a New York antiques show. The FBI, which had been alerted, seized the mask, then brought to New York the eighty-six-year-old leader of the Badger Clan, the one responsible for the Bean Dance. The mask had not been actively used since 1927, and the old man was now seeing it at the antiques show for only the second time in sixty years. Since 1927 it had been stored in a special chamber with many other sacred masks, rattles, and pots so that they could be communally fed and blessed.

When the old man went to identify the mask he found it encased in a bolted box. Seeing it locked in an airtight box unable to "breathe" brought tears to his eyes. He unlocked the box and "fed" the spirit the sacred cornmeal he carried in a pouch around his neck.

The feds seized the mask and kept it for several years as material evidence but eventually decided not to prosecute anyone connected with the theft. It could never be proven that the mask was stolen because no stolen-property report had ever been filed. The Hopi don't file them because they don't like to prosecute one another. They also keep quiet because they really don't expect non-Indians to understand that these are not just art objects and commodities but living spirits.

This kind of theft occurs frequently. In 1991, a cache of sacred Hopi objects stolen from Oraibi in 1978 were put up for sale at Sotheby's annual Indian arts sale. Sotheby's sold them in spite of tribal objections, because the "owner" claimed that since a stolen-property report was never filed, they were his.

Fortunately, those masks were bought by Elizabeth Sackler, a collector, for the sole purpose of returning them to the Hopi. She said it was the right thing to do.

As for the Wupamo, the legal authorities finally returned it to the Hopi religious leaders after many years. This living representation of God's spirit was brought home to the mask's ritual mother, the head of the Parrot Clan, whose responsibility it was to care for it.

▲

In the stark desolate beauty of the Tusayan Plateau, in a village a thousand years old, the Parrot Clan mother chants prayers. In a ceremony from this timeless spiritual world of the Hopi, her words mingle with the penetrating sounds of reggae music from a pickup truck. Its teenage inhabitants, already drunk, are parked in front of a bootlegger's house not more than twenty yards from her.

The old Badger Clan chief who first blessed the Wupamo in New York moves toward them. Seeing the old man approach, they put their beer cans down behind them. After a brief exchange they turn the music off and return with him to the blessing place. They stand quietly by his side. One of the young men is his grandson.

At the truck he says: "I will soon be gone from the world, Grandson. I have nothing to give you, no inheritance, no money, but I do have a trust fund. It's over here." He drags the boy into the circle of the Parrot Clan mother's prayers. Pointing at it, he leans over to his grandson.

"This is my trust, 'this way'—'this way' will give you life. Everything else you think you have or want will go away—your truck, the bootlegger. This is your life right here in that Spirit Friend, in these prayers. This is the life of your family. If you give it away you will give up the spirit of your people."

There are tears in the boy's eyes, so I know the spirit in the mask still lives.

▲

EPILOGUE

It doesn't matter how long your spirit lies dormant and unused. One day you hear a song, look at an object, or see a vision, and you feel its presence. It can't be bought, traded, or annihilated, because its power comes from its story.

No one can steal your spirit; you have to give it away. You can also take it back.

Find yours.

ACKNOWLEDGMENTS

———————————————▲———————————————

These friends and relatives and others unnamed have accompanied
me on this journey. They have been at my side or in my heart. To each
of you, my thanks, love, and blessings for your contributions to my life:
Judy Hammerschlag, Harrington and Andrea Luna, Dallas DeLowe,
Mona Polacca, Jerry Nelson, Zalman Schacter-Shalomi, Howie and
Sharona Silverman, Nelson Fernandez, Stan and Betty Mayersohn, Jay
Shapiro, Pam Cummings, Lynn Jackel, Vanessa Reuman, Scott and
Julie Ford, John Koriath, Joyce Mills, Billy Frank, Jr., Janet McCloud,
Gail Larsen, Jeff Herman, Mariam Pojefko, The Turtle Island Project,
Pia Manfré, Karen Crotty, Ron Teed, Carol Sowell, Fred Hills,
Leonard Peltier, and my patients.

To all my relations
Mi takuye oyacin

———————————————▲———————————————

*This book is printed on commercially grown paper
with two trees planted for every one used.*

To receive information about Dr. Hammerschlag's workshops, retreats, and lectures, or to order his tapes, please contact him at the following address:

3104 East Camelback Road, #614
Phoenix, Arizona 85016
Phone: (602) 468-1141
Fax: (602) 954-8560